Bartenders, Preachers and Golf Pros

Rowe

Published by BookLocker.com, Inc., St. Petersburg, Florida.

Printed on acid-free paper.

BookLocker.com, Inc.
2021

Second Edition

DISCLAIMER

This book details the author's personal experiences with and opinions about golf.

Before you begin any sports program, or change your lifestyle in any way, you will consult your physician or other licensed healthcare practitioner to ensure that you are in good health and that the examples contained in this book will not harm you.

The author and publisher are providing this book and its contents on an "as is" basis and make no representations or warranties of any kind with respect to this book or its contents. The author and publisher disclaim all such representations and warranties, including for example warranties of merchantability and healthcare for a particular purpose. In addition, the author and publisher do not represent or warrant that the information accessible via this book is accurate, complete or current.

Except as specifically stated in this book, neither the author or publisher, nor any authors, contributors, or other representatives will be liable for damages arising out of or in connection with the use of this book. This is a comprehensive limitation of liability that applies to all damages of any kind, including (without limitation) compensatory; direct, indirect or consequential damages; loss of data, income or profit; loss of or damage to property and claims of third parties.

This book provides content related to topics physical health issues. As such, use of this book implies your acceptance of this disclaimer.

Dedication

To Dylan, Pierce, and Jude: You guys are my greatest achievement. Each of you has special talents and will do great things someday. Follow your dreams and work hard, and you can achieve anything!

To Mom and Dad: Thank you for your support and your love. Mom, you showed me a work ethic at a young age, and it has paid dividends throughout my life. Dad, you showed me how to be a father to my boys and how to be a man in the business world.

To God, for instilling a desire and love for the game of golf and the blessings it has given me.

Forward

HOW DID THE book title *Bartenders, Preachers, and Golf Pros* come about? When thinking about the title of this book, it occurred to me that I'm always telling members that golf pros are like bartenders for successful people, and they are like preachers from a counseling perspective. Bartenders have heard every heartache from their patrons and could probably finish the story of the brokenhearted telling them the story. Golf professionals are much the same way when it comes to hearing stories about business deals. I've been doing this a long time and have been very blessed to have spent the past twenty-four years listening to successful people tell me how they made their fortune— and sometimes, how they lost it. It has always been interesting to me that people share this information on the golf course or lesson tee with golf professionals, but they do. The preacher aspect of the title happens when you have a young student open up about his struggles at home or school. The opportunity to help guide young golfers with life lessons or an adult thinking about major changes in their life is a blessing. The lesson tee isn't just a place to learn golf but actually an opportunity to make a difference in someone's life.

People tell me all the time that I have the greatest job, and it's hard to argue with them. There's not a better office in the world than the gates I drive through every day at Whispering Pines. This book was written to tell stories and hopefully help your golf game, with a few life lessons thrown in along the way.

— Chris Rowe

The 16th at the Olympic Club

FOR MY OLDEST son's Christmas gift, I decided it was better to create a memory than to buy an actual gift. Dylan is in the professional golf management program at Sam Houston State University and had been asking me about a golf trip for months. I made a call to my good friend Alan Dunckel to make arrangements for a tee time at the Olympic Club and also invited one of my members, Stan Whitfill, to round out our foursome. We caught a flight the day after Christmas and headed to California. The Olympic Club in San Francisco, site of numerous US Opens, is one of my favorite golf courses in the world. The magnificent clubhouse, spectacular routing of holes, and strategic greens make the golf course an obvious choice for major championships.

When we arrived, the weather could not have been better! One of the traditions of the Olympic Club is their burger dog. Even though it was only ten o'clock in the morning, my stomach was set on Texas time, and that meant lunchtime. We walked over to the driving range and ordered the famous burger dog with pickles, ketchup, mustard, and relish ... It doesn't matter how many times I eat one of those, they always taste amazing. After a quick brunch, we hit some golf balls to loosen up and then made our way to the first tee.

The first hole is a par-five downhill with the tee box sitting directly in front of the pro shop window. It's always a little nerve-racking standing on this tee, knowing a bunch of golf pros are watching you hit your drive. Fortunately, I ripped one down the middle, and we were off to the races. Dylan and I were having so much fun playing this great golf course and spending time with Alan and Stan.

When we reached the back nine, it seemed like the proper thing to do to order another burger dog, which tasted just as good as the burger dog earlier. The back nine at the Olympic Club is a very stern test, but very fair. The hardest hole on the entire golf course is the 16th par-five. We had been discussing the hole throughout the round. Alan had marshaled during the US Open the last time it was played at the Olympic Club and had a lot of inside knowledge about that week.

The Olympic Club is known for golfers collapsing coming down the stretch of the major championships. Ben Hogan had lost to an unknown in the 50s, Arnold Palmer had blown a huge lead on the final nine holes, along with many others faltering on the back nine to lose. The last major championship at the Olympic Club had Jim Furyk leading on the back nine. When Furyk arrived at the 16th hole, the tee box had been moved up considerably from where it had been the previous days of the tournament. Furyk, walking off the 15th green, realized the tee box had been moved and was visibly puzzled. The USGA had put in a new back tee box to create extra yardage for this mammoth par-five. The last day of the US Open, their thinking was to move the tee box up to the members' tee, some eighty yards ahead, and allow the players the chance to possibly reach the green in two shots. Jim Furyk, knowing his length probably wouldn't allow him to reach this green in two shots, proceeded to tee up his golf ball and hit one of the worst shots in US Open history. His tee shot snapped violently left, going into very a tall and heavily vegetated area of trees.

Jim Furyk's opportunity to win the US Open was lost on the 16th, as he never recovered. During his press conference, he admitted that he couldn't get comfortable and never thought the tee box would be moved that far up for the final round. His story was replayed in full detail from the 14th hole until we arrived at the 16th to Stan. Alan gave details of what the day had been like during that final round of the US Open as Stan listened to every detail, like a child listening to their grandpa telling a story.

As we walked off the 15th green, Dylan and I walked toward the back tee. Alan noted the US Open tee box was no longer there, but pointed in the direction of where the USGA had placed it. Stan asked where Jim Furyk had played his shot from, and Alan said, "From the tee box we are going to play."

After Dylan and I hit our tee shots, we walked up to where Stan and Alan were playing their shot. Stan asked again about where Jim Furyk had hit the ball during the US Open. Alan pointed to the area where Jim Furyk's ball had ended up, about 180 yards straight left. Stan addressed his ball and with a violent swing, snap-hooked his shot into the exact place where Jim Furyk had put his shot. I literally could not contain myself and was laughing out loud. Stan had been so inquisitive about what Jim Furyk had done on this hole that he had actually hit the same shot! We laughed all the way down the fairway! If there was ever a self-fulfilling prophecy, Stan had performed it.

As we reached the 18th green, we took off our hats to shake hands, as we all knew it had truly been an amazing day in San Francisco.

The lesson behind this story is the same as what psychologist tell us: We become what we think. Many times when we see or think about something bad happening, it usually does. How many times have you missed a short putt and immediately said, "I knew I was going to miss it." We do this all the time when we play golf. If Jim Furyk would've backed off and thought to himself that the hole was actually easier now, he probably would have won the tournament. If we say, "Don't hit it in the water," what do we usually do? We hit it in the water!

If we would've told Stan that Jim Furyk had hit a great tee shot and birdied the hole—or not mentioned it at all—I'm willing to bet Stan's shot would not have had the poor result. Personally, I'm glad Stan hit the shot, because needling him and giving him a hard time was so much fun. It also made for a great story for my students to help them understand the power of the mind.

The next time you're faced with a shot and you don't have good thoughts, back off, restart, and get a good picture of a great shot in your mind *before* hitting the ball.

Looking back on Christmas and birthdays, there are very few gifts I've remembered receiving, but I've never forgotten a family vacation or golf trip with friends. You can *buy* gifts, but you *make* memories. Go make some memories this year with your friends and loved ones, and if you ever find yourself on the 16th at Olympic, remember this story.

Eighteen Chapters

WHEN WRITING MY first book, *He Who Looks Up Shall See a Bad Shot*, I didn't write chapters, but told short stories. Most books you read have chapters, just like most golf courses have eighteen holes. I like to tell my students that every golf course is a book of golf holes made up of eighteen chapters. If a college student had a test after reading a book, they should know the details and highlights about each chapter. All the chapters of the book are important, but some are more important than others.

Your college professor goes over a specific chapter and says, "You might want to read this chapter more than once." The test always has more questions from that chapter than some of the others chapters reviewed.

On the golf course, there are always key holes you need to pay more attention to than others. All the holes are important and require you to "read" through them, so to speak. Par fives usually could be a more important chapter because the second shot challenges you to make a decision. Do you go for the green in two? If you lay up, what yardage do you lay up for your third shot? The rest of the holes require decisions as well, so never skip over chapters and assume you will not be tested on them.

When you play your home course, you should know every detail of every hole. If asked to open your home course book to chapter twelve, you should be able to tell me exactly how you would play that hole. You should be able to tell me every detail about the layout of the hole, the complexity of the green, and the best angle to approach the green. If you are preparing for a tournament on a different course, you should study every detail and be prepared to get a call from your golf professor asking you how you would play each hole.

In 2004, I was fortunate enough to work with Kevin Muncrief at all three stages of PGA Qualifying School. I'll never forget walking all the holes at Orange County National and studying every detail of each hole. We both studied all thirty-six chapters extensively. When Kevin played the tournament, he knew how he would play every hole when he stepped on the tee box. He didn't have to think about or guess—he already knew. The studying paid off, and he qualified for his PGA Tour card!

Golf courses are books, and holes are chapters. Pay attention in class and study each chapter. Your test is the club championship, member guest, state qualifier, or your Saturday morning game. You should know all the chapters when you arrive at the first tee and make an A+ on your next eighteen-hole exam!

100 Percent—50 Percent—25 Percent

THIS IS A wonderful drill for your next practice session. Your full swing is 100 percent, your half swing is 50 percent, and your baby swing is 25 percent. If you hit your seven iron 160 yards, then your 50 percent swing obviously would be 80 yards and your 25 percent swing would be 40 yards.

Try and warm up this way the next time you go to the range, starting at 25 percent. When your swing reaches 100 percent and you start hitting the ball poorly, it's time to drop down to 50 percent. If you still hit the ball poorly at 50 percent, drop down to your 25 percent swing. When you start hitting the ball well with your 25 percent swing, work up to your 50 percent swing and eventually back to 100 percent.

This drill not only gets your tempo better but also syncs your body with the club. When the club and body are synchronized, you're creating optimum clubhead speed.

Try this drill, and you will hit the ball farther and more consistently, guaranteed!

Accidents

HAVE YOU EVER noticed that most accidents on the ski slopes happen toward the end of the day? One of the rules we have as a family when skiing in Park City is to not go up for "one more run" at the end of the day if we are too tired. When you've skied all day and your legs are tired, you have more of a chance of taking a fall than at the beginning of the day when your legs are rested.

This happens to golfers on the practice range, as well. As you get tired, your body doesn't respond like it did earlier in the practice session. When you get tired on the range, flaws start to find their way into your swing, and next thing you know, you are hitting the ball all over the place. Give yourself enough time to accomplish your goals on the range, but don't go too long and take a fall on the "slopes," so to speak.

Lost Keys

ALL OF US have lost our keys at some point. It's usually at the worst time, but when is there really a good time to lose anything? I'm not a forgetful person, but I do admit to losing my keys every once in a while. When this happens, I usually find myself running all over the house, looking in places where I usually leave them. Sometimes, as George Carlin used to say, "We look in the same place more than once, like they are magically going to appear, even though we just looked in the exact spot two minutes before." Eventually, the keys are found by retracing our steps and working backward. Numerous times, we find them in a place where we did something unusual, like hitting a bump while driving in a golf cart and having the keys fall out of the cart. Other times, we can't find them because we set them down in a different place than normal. If we retrace our steps, though, we can usually find where we did something different or unusual that caused the misplacement.

When we have a bad hole on the golf course, we should use the same principle as when we misplace our keys. Look back at the path you've taken from the green all the way back to the tee box. When you do this, you can pinpoint where your mistake was made, and it's usually not where you think! I always ask students, after they have a poor score on a hole, "Where did you make your mistake?" They almost always say, "The missed putt," or, "The drive that missed the fairway." After we go through all the shots from the green to the tee, we often find it was the poor chip that caused the putt to be outside a comfortable distance to make. The drive turned out wasn't the problem, but the poor decision they made resulted in a big number on the scorecard.

Remember, the place where you think you lost your shots usually isn't the place you actually lost them. Look where you know you've been, and retrace your steps to find your keys. Use this philosophy on the course, and you will find your game!

Balance

ONE THING ALL professional athletes have in common is balance. Basketball players shoot the ball with balance, football players position themselves on the line of scrimmage balanced, and baseball players set up in the batter's box in a balanced position. Good balance doesn't guarantee a good shot, but poor balance absolutely hurts your ability to hit consistent good shots.

I've used different examples of balance throughout my teaching career. You can imagine yourself on a surfboard out in the ocean while making golf swings and trying to stay on the board. I've told students to imagine standing on a floating log in one of our water hazards with gators swimming around them. All of these images are good for staying balanced throughout your golf swing.

Today, I gave a lesson to a young man who was having a difficult time keeping his balance. He would make a beautiful backswing but fall forward after almost every shot. I started looking around and realized the wall behind us was the perfect width and height for this article. I've given thousands of lessons with this wall behind me but never thought to use it for a balance drill. I made the young man stand on the wall and actually make swings. If he lost his balance, he would fall at least four feet to the next tee box.

He made beautiful swings and kept his balance without falling off the wall. We then went to the lower level and started hitting balls again. His balance had improved tremendously after only a few swings on the wall.

Next time you find yourself losing your balance, put this image in your mind, and I guarantee you will keep your balance!

Stuck

Frame 1: Perfect Address Position	Frame 2: Stuck!	Frame 3: Proper Path

We've all heard the term *stuck*. Here is what *stuck* looks like (frame 2). If you start your downswing and hit the bench, you are *stuck*. Good players have the tendency to get the club behind them and have to flip their hands through the impact zone to square the face.

Frame 3 shows what staying on top of the ball would look like with a proper downswing path. If your golf ball starts out to the right and your tendency is blocks or big right-to-left hooks, imagine a bench between you and your golf ball. Don't hit the bench, but continue to rotate your body through the impact zone, and you will never be *stuck* again!

Bounce, Bounce, Shoot

───────── ❧ ─────────

THE BEST WEEK in sports is approaching, with the NCAA Tournament under way and the Masters just around the corner. Obviously, all of you who know me know I'm cheering for the Sooners to hopefully win it all. As I was giving a lesson yesterday to a young golfer, I told him that the routine is the most important part of putting. I've said before that anyone can putt! People win cars on *The Price Is Right* by holing a putt! My ten-year-old can two putt from twenty feet if I tell him an ice cream bar is on the line if he can do it.

All of us have a chance to even beat Jordan Spieth in a putting contest if we were to challenge him on the putting green. (I did say a *chance*—but not a probability!)

The one thing every good putter and every good free-throw shooter have in common is their routine. Watch the NCAA Tournament and notice the best free-throw shooters all have a routine they repeat every time. They take the same amount of dribbles, look at the basket, and shoot. They don't hesitate or vary from their routines.

On Masters Week, watch Jordan, Jason, and Rory go through their putting routines. Each of them will take practice strokes, look at the hole, and stroke. The best players do this regardless of the situation.

The NCAA Tournament will most likely have a moment in the final minutes of the game where a foul is committed and the player will shoot a free throw. Watch to see if the player's routine changes from the beginning of the game to the final minutes. When you are watching the Masters, pay attention to see if the leaders change their routine on the back nine at Augusta on Sunday. I will guarantee the winner will have the same putting routine on the first hole of the tournament as he has on the last hole.

Your putting routine should be like this:

- Makes strokes looking at hole with a free-flowing motion.
- Address the putter behind ball.
- Take one look at the hole and slowly move your eyes back to ball.
- Stroke putt.
- Your head stays still for two seconds before you look.

Do this every time, and I promise your putting average will get better!

Breathe Out

DURING THE PGA Merchandise Show, you see everything you could imagine in the golf industry. One of the most unique items this year was from FlightScope. FlightScope is a Doppler radar that tracks your golf ball's spin rate, distance, carry, club path, angle of attack, and many more details. This is incredible technology, and everyone should hit shots with their instructor using this device.

FlightScope added a new technology this year that includes a headband that reads your brain waves after each shot. You place the band on your head, and the screen it's connected with either shows green or red. If the screen shows red, you have tension in your swing. If the screen is green, your tension level is good.

As the headband was placed on my head, the screen turned red immediately. Feeling a bit ridiculous wearing a suit with this headband on and the screen turning red wasn't a surprise. The person who invented this technology was standing next to me, and he asked me to hit a ball. The PGA Merchandise Show actually has a driving range set up where you can hit all the new clubs from each manufacturer. They handed me a nine iron, and the shot soared into the back of the net seventy yards away. Feeling pretty good about the shot, I immediately turned to look at the data. The data showed green at address and then went to red as the golf swing began.

After a few more shots with the exact same results, I decided to try and trick the machine. I've never taken a lie detector test, but this technology works in a similar way. Earlier in the day, the proponent group had had numerous classes for golf instructors to get continuing education. I absolutely love attending anything that gives me new ideas and makes me a better instructor. One of the classes was a mental class taught by a sports psychologist. The main objective of his class was breathing techniques to relieve tension. "Do you breathe in on your backswing or out?" We've all heard the joke, but there is validity to the question. When you let all the air out of your lungs, you start to relax. This seemed like the perfect time to try this technique with a headband filled with sensors and a screen that wouldn't turn green. I addressed the ball and took a deep breath just before pulling the club back, and then let all the air out of my lungs. The inventor of this technology looked at me and said, "That was good!" The screen had turned green at the moment my lungs were exhaling.

This got me thinking about what the sports psychologist had been talking about. What if you inhale when addressing the ball and exhale at the start of the swing? Every shot hit after my new breathing technique produced a green screen!

When we get under pressure or get nervous on the golf course, we tend to speed up our swings and have tension throughout our body. If you breathe using this technique, it immediately relaxes your body and eliminates tension. I'm not saying do this on every shot, but try it when you're on the first tee and nervous, or standing over a putt to shoot your lowest score. It worked for me at the PGA Merchandise Show, and it will work for you the next time you're on the links!

Bunker Shots Made Easy

—— ❧ ——

GROWING UP PLAYING Tishomingo Golf Course was interesting (to say the least). The golf course is a nine-hole public course in Oklahoma. The course had no bunkers, crowned greens, and the usual gangsome that would never let you play through. The best thing about the course was its location. My house was a five-minute three-wheeler ride through the trails on a back road, cut across a path, and drive up the third hole on the cart trail to grab my golf cart. The golf course was my sanctuary! It didn't matter if it wasn't the greatest course; it was a place where I could get in my golf cart and play golf all morning, go to my grandpa's Dairy Queen and have a cheeseburger for lunch, and then return and play until dinner.

Returning to the course while visiting family, memories still come back to me of how much was learned on these holes. Without this course, my career path most likely would have been different, and I'm very thankful for those nine holes.

The one shot that wasn't available at Tishomingo Golf Course was the bunker shot, because there were no bunkers anywhere. It took being in a bunker with the lead in the Oak Hills Junior Invitational for me to realize the need for a bunker lesson. After chunking, skulling, and finally making a large number, the tournament was lost because of my lack of knowledge on how to play the shot correctly.

Dornick Hills Country Club, which my dad later joined, was thirty miles away and was one of the top-ranked courses in Oklahoma. Making a call to the golf professional at Dornick Hills was my first step to learning how to hit out of the sand. He showed me the proper technique and simplified the process. This inspired me to master bunkers shots.

I actually became infatuated with hitting bunker shots. Reading Seve Ballesteros's book *Natural Golf* a dozen times helped me take information and come up with my own technique. The next step was building a bunker at my house. My dad had some railroad ties for landscaping that stood about three feet tall and bordered the yard. The obvious choice to dump a bunch of sand was right at the base of the railroad ties. If the bunker shot wasn't hit properly, the ball would hit the railroad ties and come right back at me. This was a very good lesson on how to get the ball out of sand very quickly, or the failure to do so would hurt for weeks.

Here is a checklist for great bunker shots:

- Ball position, center of stance.
- Clubface always points at target, regardless of how open the face is at address.
- Majority of weight on left foot.
- Squat legs and butt at address.
- Hinge wrist quickly and steep.
- Hold wrist angle all the way through impact.
- Impact sand as close to ball as possible.
- *Face* to *face*: Finish with the face of the club pointing toward your face.

Hopefully, this helps you with your bunker shots. It is my favorite part of the game to teach. There are so many other bunker shots I could write about, but this simple outline of the basic principles should help you look like Seve the next time you are in a bunker.

Change Up Your Practice Session

WHEN YOU PRACTICE your short game, make sure you don't become one-dimensional. Most people take a few balls and hit shots from the same place, then leave feeling like they've had a good practice session. Short-game practice should encompass numerous shots you might encounter in a round. If you hit the same short over and over from a perfect lie, you will probably get pretty good at that particular shot, but rarely do you get that exact lie and shot on the course. Mix it up. Take six balls and throw them to areas around the green and play them as they lie. Make this even more challenging by putting every ball out and not moving on to the next shot without getting that one up and down. Don't make it easy, and don't make it too difficult. Throw balls around the green in the areas you would be most prone to find your ball in an actual round. I guarantee that if you get all six balls up and down, you will lower your scores and have more fun on the course!

Clifford and Ben Hogan

My GOLF CAREER has introduced me to so many incredible people throughout the past thirty-one years playing and working as a PGA professional. I've hung out with the president of the United States and played golf with hall of fame athletes, along with numerous famous musicians. I've been blessed to work at Colonial and Whispering Pines the past twenty-one years, and you bump into a lot of great people along the way.

When I worked at Colonial, our shifts usually had the assistant professional opening the golf shop three days a week and closing the other three days. The mornings when I opened, there would always be this particular caddy on the corner of Colonial Parkway, waiting for someone to give him a ride. The caddy's name was Clifford. I never knew his last name but made a habit of giving him a ride to the clubhouse. The public bus would drop him off on University Street, and he would walk halfway to the clubhouse about the time I would arrive at the back gate entrance near the fourth tee.

For years, I would have brief conversations during our two-minute drive. We always had small talk, and I always wished him a good day on the links. One day, I asked Clifford if he had ever shagged golf balls for Ben Hogan. To my surprise, he nodded. When you work at Colonial for a decade, you hear every Hogan story imaginable. I never met Mr. Hogan, and to this day, I wish I'd made my way over to Shady Oaks while he was still alive.

I asked Clifford what it was like to shag balls for Hogan. Shagging golf balls is when a person takes a leather satchel of roughly sixty balls and hits them to the person standing at different distances. The golfer hitting the balls would motion for the person shagging to move farther or closer as he changed clubs. The better the player, the less the person shagging had to move.

Mr. Hogan was legendary for hitting balls that would one hop to the person shagging as he would catch them in a towel and drop them in the shag bag. Clifford began to tell me about Mr. Hogan going to the right side of the tenth hole at Colonial and hitting balls across the 10th and 18th fairways while Clifford stood in the 17th fairway. These three holes run parallel at Colonial, and back then, golf courses didn't have the elaborate driving ranges we have today.

I asked Clifford, "How good was Mr. Hogan?"

He said, "Everything people said about Mr. Hogan was true!" He said, "You move a step here and a step there, and the balls would land right next to the shag bag."

Clifford then told me the line I'll never forget! In a southern drawl, he said, "Chris, there were numerous times the golf balls would bounce right in the shag bag."

I smiled and said, "You swear that really happened."

He grinned real big with numerous teeth missing and said, "It happened all the time. He was that good!"

What I would have done to see Mr. Hogan hit some of those shots. I'll never forget those drives up the Colonial Parkway with Clifford riding next to me.

Closest to the Hole

We RECENTLY HOSTED our annual Robertson Cup Invitational. The tournament is comprised of one club professional, along with three amateurs for three days at Whispering Pines Golf Club. All the par-three holes have a closest-to-the-hole prize for the professionals, along with a Rolex watch for any hole-in-one. Each professional has a chance to win $500 if he hits his shot the closest to the hole during that round.

Before the tournament began, I told my assistant professionals that if my shot won a closest-to-the-hole, they would receive half my winnings. My assistants worked a tremendous amount of hours during this event and deserved a bonus if their boss was fortunate enough to hit a shot close enough to beat out the other professionals.

The first round of the tournament began on a cool Monday morning in April. The greens were lightning-quick, and the pins were tucked in some precarious positions. Whispering Pines has four par-three holes, so there would be four opportunities every round to win. When our group arrived at the first par-three, I noticed how my focus had intensified on the tee box. The pin was in a back-left area of the green, which required a high fade to have any chance of keeping the ball close. My club selection was a six iron from 184 yards. The shot came off perfectly, and the ball soared toward the pin with a slight fade, stopping ten feet from the hole. When we arrived at the green, it was evident my ball was the closest to the hole at that point. I wrote my name on the proximity marker and placed it where my ball had come to rest. After the round, my assistants were thrilled with their boss for hitting the closest shot of the morning round on that par-three.

The second round started in the afternoon, and I arrived once again to the hole where my shot had claimed the prize five hours earlier. My mindset this time was *I've already hit this shot closer today than anyone in the field. Why not do it again!*

The choice of club was the same, and the result was even better, with the ball coming to rest five feet from the hole. When the second round concluded, my assistants were once again happy with their boss. The shot had held up, and I had won the closest-to-the-hole for a second time on the same par-three.

When you have a prize on the line, you tend to focus more than when you don't have something on the line. In this case, it was a double bonus for me, because I really wanted my assistants to financially benefit from the shot. I noticed that my routine was the same as the rest of the day, but my focus had increased considerably. Many times during a golf lesson, I will give my student five shots to hole out a shot from one hundred yards or chip one in on the chipping green to a particular hole. If they can accomplish the shot, they will receive a dozen balls. It's interesting to watch how much the students concentrate on these shots versus the shots earlier in the lesson. I often joke with them about needing golf balls when I see how focused they become. It's rare that they make the shot, but they always seem to hit the ball closer when they are trying to hole the shot versus hitting it close.

I've got a saying: "If you try to get close to your target and you don't, you probably will not be close." The second part of this saying is "If you try to hole the shot and don't, you're probably going to be close." My agenda on all of the par-three holes was to make a hole-in-one for a Rolex watch, and if I didn't succeed, my shot would probably be closer to the hole. So the question is, Why do we not try to make every shot and have this type of focus every time we hit a shot into a green?

Tour players go through precise routines, visualizing every detail about their shots. Their proximity to the hole is much better than amateurs, and I believe this mindset is part of the reason. The next round you play, try and make every shot within one hundred yards, and try to make a hole-in-one on every par-three. The odds are against you holing out, but I guarantee you will be a lot closer to the hole than you would be otherwise.

Cut Off the Fat in Your Swing

———— ✐ ————

HAVE YOU EVER had a steak that had a big chunk of fat on it? If you were at a nice restaurant, you probably would send the steak back to the kitchen. If you were at home, you would probably cut the fat off and eat only the meat. (Rib-eye steaks will be excluded in this story.)

This illustration is used at least once a week when I'm teaching a student about shortening their swing. When the backswing becomes too long, numerous things can happen, and the majority of the time, it is not good! I honestly can't count the number of times I've asked a student to make a backswing and stop just past their pocket, and then show them on video where they actually stopped. What we feel and what is real are never the same in golf swings. Almost every time, the student can't believe what they are seeing on video. Their backswing stops very close to parallel when they feel like they only went halfway back. I call this "cutting off the fat" in the golf swing.

Fat is no good on your body—or in your golf swing! When you take the 20 percent extra that is not needed in the swing, you get all meat. When you don't have the access, you don't have to compensate as much to make the downswing.

The next time you go out to the range, try and make a half swing and have someone film you with their iPhone. I will bet you will be surprised at where you actually stop your club.

The next time you order a steak and there is big chunk of fat, remember this golf lesson, but don't complain to the chef—if your significant other cooked it!

Disconnect and Connect

Last month, I took my father and my oldest son to the Masters in Augusta, Georgia. If you are a golfer and haven't done this, it needs to go on your bucket list. I've been very blessed to go many times, but never had my dad and oldest son, Dylan, accompany me.

When you arrive at the Masters, everyone (and I mean *everyone*) has the look of a kid seeing his presents under the tree on Christmas morning. Most people who have attended on numerous occasions have a routine when they enter the gates. First, you hit the merchandise tent and purchase for your friends, family, and yourself. I'm in the golf business, know what everything costs, and still spend $600 on T-shirts and hats. You then go and purchase a pimento-cheese sandwich. I don't care for pimento cheese, but staying with tradition, I eat half a sandwich to say I ate one.

Another great tradition is the placement of your personal chair. Everyone writes their name on the back of their chair and places it near the green or tee box they want to watch. You can leave for hours and return to your chair at any time during the day.

The Masters also charges two dollars for a sandwich and one dollar for a drink. You can have a great meal for under six dollars, where other tournaments charge eight dollars for a hot dog and ten dollars for a beer. The Masters does it right, and without question, they run the greatest tournament in the world.

As we went through the entrance that day, they had metal detectors and were screening everyone like they were going through airport security. The Masters has a no cell phone policy, and there are no exceptions. On practice-round days, you are allowed to bring cameras, but pictures can't be taken with a cell phone. As we walked the magnificent grounds of Augusta, I started to notice that I hadn't called or sent a text to anyone for hours. The patrons were all talking and having conversations while waiting on the next group of players to come through. The golf world is small, and I bumped into Whispering Pines members, along with members from other clubs I knew. I even struck up a conversation with a guy from Ohio, and we talked about the Oklahoma vs. Ohio State game back in the 70s, where my friend Bud Hebert was the holder for the game-winning kick to beat Ohio State. To my surprise, this guy was at that game forty years ago and remembered every detail.

My son and I talked about so many things that day. The entire twelve hours flew by so fast, and that's when I realized that not once had I seen a cell phone. Not having a cell phone forces you to talk to people face-to-face. At one point, I was standing on the 14th tee and realized that all of us, me included, would have been texting or talking to someone on our phones until the next group came through. Instead, people were getting to know each other and having meaningful conversations.

As for me, it was an incredible day with my father and son. I'm glad we were not allowed to bring in cell phones, because it allowed me to have one of the best days of my life with family.

The next time you are with your family, put the cell phones away. Tell the family you are going to have a "Masters Evening" at the house.

The kids will be fine not playing their video game or texting their buddies. Your wife can go one evening without texting her girlfriends, and your work will still be there tomorrow even if you don't respond to every email.

Thank you Augusta National for making me leave my cell phone in the car on that beautiful April day in Georgia!

Don't Make the Moment Bigger than It Really Is

IF YOU WERE asked to walk ten feet across a two-by-four board that was five feet above the ground, would you be able to do it? I'm guessing most of you would be able to. Now, what if the board was raised to fifteen feet above the ground? Most of you might say this would be harder or scarier, but the truth is the board is still the same width and length. The only difference is the height that the board has been raised. But it's still the same ten-foot-long two-by-four.

Many times when we are hitting a golf shot, we make the moment bigger than it actually is. Is a birdie putt easier than a triple-bogey putt? No. They are exactly the same because each putt counts the same. We often put more pressure on ourselves when we are playing a famous hole or have a putt to win a bet. Every shot counts one stroke, regardless of the moment.

A few months ago, I was playing the 8th hole at Pebble Beach. My tee shot landed on the right side of the fairway and was in perfect position. Those of you who have played Pebble Beach and stood on top of the cliff know how spectacular the moment can be. As I looked down at the green with a 360-degree panorama view of the most beautiful place on Earth, it was hard to imagine the shot not being a big moment. Jack Nicklaus says the second shot on the 8th hole at Pebble Beach is the best second shot in golf, and as I stood there with a seven iron in my hand, Jack's statement entered my mind. I started to think about how beautiful the ocean and cliffs were—and how cool it would be to tell the guys I birdied the 8th hole at Pebble Beach. I really wanted to hit the shot perfect!

With all the distractions, I collected my thoughts and went through my routine. As I stood over the ball, I told myself, *This shot is just another golf shot.* My mind cleared, and my focus was on making a good swing. The ball took off toward the green and gently faded toward the flag. Holding my pose and knowing the shot had been struck perfectly, I watched the ball land softly on the green ten feet from the hole. Unfortunately, the putt didn't go in, but the greatest second shot in golf was hit perfectly.

The point of this story is to understand that no shot is more important than any other shot. It's important to go through your routine and make a swing like you make on the driving range. The next time you are playing a famous golf course or have the opportunity to do something special on your home course, remember to not let the moment get too big. Every shot counts exactly the same, and no moment is bigger than another.

Embarrassment at Church

ANYONE WHO READS my articles knows I love music. If Van Halen called tomorrow, I wouldn't quit my job at Whispering Pines, but I would love to get on stage with those guys and rock out! So many years ago, when I was playing in my band Built for Speed, I would practice a bit on the drums. I was the lead singer and played guitar, but never was very good at keeping a beat. This is why I wasn't the drummer!

The problem with me is that I thought I could play drums. When we finished practice, I would get on my buddy's drum set and pound away. I knew my playing wasn't great, but thought I could keep a beat. One night at church, the drummer didn't show up. Yes, you guessed it: I walked up to the drum set and told the pianist I was going to fill in. The first song began, and I started playing. Have you ever felt that hot streak run up the back of your spine when you realized you were in trouble? As I was trying to keep the beat, I looked out in the crowd and saw my horrified mother looking at me with embarrassment. She couldn't save me, and I couldn't get off the stage fast enough. The pianist looked at me and wondered, *What in the world is he doing?*

The truth was, I should have never gotten on stage and tried to play drums! I could have played a guitar because I played guitar all the time, but the drums were not my area of expertise. I've never lacked confidence, and humility is a hard pill to swallow, and I've made a habit out of embarrassing myself.

In golf, many times we get ourselves in the same situation. We think we can pull off a shot we haven't practiced. We play the back tees when we don't have the length to play them. We get in bets over our head that we shouldn't be in. We try and hit the miracle shots when we are in the woods, rather than taking the easy punch back into the fairway shot. All this to say that I did this (played drums) in front of an entire congregation and absolutely crashed and burned. When you're on the course and you're faced with a shot you haven't practiced, don't try and create a miracle. Stick with what you're comfortable with. If you are not the best chipper, then putt from off the green when you have the opportunity. If the hole you're playing is a dogleg left and you don't draw the ball, hit your standard shot and choose a line that fits your shot. If you know your bunker game is not the best, don't challenge the tight pin tucked next to the bunker … You get the picture!

The next time you're faced with an uncomfortable shot, remember me, Chris Rowe, trying to play the drums during a Sunday night church service, and stick with what you're comfortable with! It will be the best decision every time.

Fill Up Your Tank

WOULD YOU EVER stop to get gas and only put 75 percent in the tank if you knew that amount of gas wouldn't get you to your destination? I'm guessing none of you have ever done this—or least *hope* none of you have. How many times have you pulled out a seven iron on the range, knowing it wouldn't reach the target you were aiming for on the range? This has probably happened to every one of you at some point! Why would you not take enough club? It amazes me how many times this happens while walking up and down the range, giving tips.

If the target you are aiming for takes an eight iron to reach, don't hit a nine iron. When you do this, you are doing yourself a disservice because you would never do this on the golf course. Of course, you might pick the wrong club during a round and come up short or hit long of the target, but on the driving range, you have a controlled environment. After you've hit a few shots on the range, it's very easy to grab another club to reach your intended target. If you continue to hit a club that doesn't reach your target, you will subconsciously start swinging harder because you see the ball landing short.

The next time you go to the range, pick the club that actually reaches your target. When you change targets, make sure the club you choose reaches that target. When you practice this way, you are simulating what it's going to be like on the golf course. Practice like you want to play, and you will play like you practice!

Fix a Flat

WE'VE ALL HAD this happen at some point in our lives. We walk out and look at our car and notice that one of the tires has very little air. Murphy's Law: We don't have any Fix-a-Flat with us, and the closest repair shop is ten miles away. You evaluate your tire to see if it's possible to make it to the repair shop without doing damage, and determine you are going to try and drive it. Would you drive your car very fast to get to the repair shop, or would you drive slowly? Obviously, you should drive slowly to avoid the tire completely tearing apart and doing damage to your wheel. If you keep your speed to a minimum, you will probably make it to the repair shop even though your tire is in bad shape.

Most of us do not have perfect golf swings. We are all flawed golfers, hacking our way through this golf universe while hoping to find the magic swing key to shoot better scores. Well, here is one magic swing tip: Slow your swing down!

If you have poor swing mechanics and swing too fast, it's much like driving really fast with a low tire. Even if you have a problem with your tire, you can drive slow enough that it will still function for a short trip. If your swing has flaws, which all of ours do, slow it down and allow your flaws to be minimized, rather than be magnified.

The moral to this story is gear your swing down until your swing mechanics are solid. When your swing mechanics are in good shape, you can swing more aggressively with more speed. There is never a problem having too much speed, as long as you have good swing mechanics. Jason Day swings very hard with a lot of speed, but his mechanics are perfect.

The next time you have low tire pressure, drive slow, and the next time you have swing issues, change the rhythm in your swing down to a slower pace.

P.S. Go buy a can of Fix-a-Flat and put it in your car today!

Forget the Last Shot

WE'VE ALL HIT a bad golf shot and carried the emotion to the next shot. This rarely results in a good shot when we are aggravated about the previous one. One of the rules for my students is to hit the reset button after every shot. When you hit a drive, you usually have a few minutes before you address the next shot. Once you leave the tee box, your mind doesn't need to think about how good or bad the shot was. The shot has already happened, and there is nothing you can do to make it better or worse. As you walk to your ball, talk to your playing partner or think about your family—whatever you think about is fine, as long as it doesn't involve the previous shot. Once you arrive at your ball, then you go into focus mode and start the process of hitting the shot.

An average round of golf takes four and a half hours, with each swing taking an average of three seconds. If you shoot eighty, that equates to two hundred and forty seconds of actual golf shots. That's a total of four minutes out of the four and a half hours on the golf course. That means you have four hours and twenty-six minutes to think about anything else besides your last shot.

Enjoy your time on the links, focus when you should focus, and think about all the great things you have in your life as you walk to your next shot!

Getting Pulled by the Tide

───── ✣ ─────

LAST MONTH, THE family vacation took place in beautiful Destin, Florida. Destin has the whitest sand and prettiest water in the United States in my opinion. The kids absolutely love hanging out at the beach, and it's a place we've visited many times over the years.

One of the major rules for my kids during any beach vacation is to find a reference point, like the hotel or a cabana, when they are in the ocean. As the boys caught wave after wave on their boogie boards, the tide moved them farther from the reference point. They had no idea they had drifted so far until they saw Dad waving at them. The tide had pulled the kids at least 150 yards as they rode wave after wave, never realizing they were drifting down the coast.

Many times, our alignment gets off, posture gets sloppy, or old habits start to resurface. This happens to all of us, and we seldom realize we are drifting down the "Golf Coast," so to speak. Your reference point should always be your swing instructor. Just like my kids were told to look back every ten minutes to see where they were in relation to our hotel, the golfer should always have their instructor take a look every few weeks to make sure their fundamentals are in line.

It doesn't take long to get off track and drift off course in this game. Your reference point is always there, so give him a call on a regular basis to make sure your game doesn't drift too far!

Giant Arms and Small Legs

HOW MANY TIMES have you seen a guy coming out of the gym or walking around the grocery store wearing a super-tight shirt to show off his muscles? Not to get weird, but how many of those guys had huge upper bodies and small lower bodies? This made me think of how out of proportion their bodies look. They don't work enough on their lower bodies to match the upper body.

In golf, this happens with short game and long game. Most of you spend all of your practice time beating balls on the range. If you are honest, the percentage of range versus short game practice is way out of proportion.

When I worked at Colonial, I always marveled at the touring professional practice sessions. The person who impressed me the most was Nick Faldo. Sir Nick showed up early Thursday morning with a late morning tee time. He was one of the first pros to get to the range that morning, where he started his practice session of going through the entire bag. After he hit balls for about an hour, he went to the short game area, where he spent another hour chipping, pitching, putting, and hitting bunker shots. He then went to the first tee and played his round.

Sir Nick was a six-time major champion, but he wasn't the dominate player at that time in his career—but he still had a balanced practice routine. After he posted his score and ate lunch, he repeated the entire practice session again before leaving the grounds. For all of you aspiring golfers who would like to play on the PGA Tour, follow this model!

The point to this story is a balanced approach to practice. If you're an incredible ball striker but can't get the ball up and down when you miss a green, you look like the big-arms-and-small-legs guy. Spend an equal amount of time in all areas of your game. Obviously, there will be days where you need to spend more time on certain parts of your game where you are struggling, but don't neglect the other areas.

Tiger Woods is a great example of this. A few years ago when he started working with Sean Foley, he spent so much time working on his ball striking that his putting suffered. Now he has rectified this and has balanced out his game (with the statistics to back it up).

If you do go to the gym, work all areas of your body so you don't look like *that* guy. In your golf game, take the balanced approach to your practice sessions, and you will see the results on the course!

"Go Annika"

─── ❈ ───

IN 2003, ANNIKA Sörenstam announced she was going to play in the Colonial National Invitation. This made national news because Annika was going to compete against the men in a PGA Tour event. Annika at the time was the best female golfer in the world and had even shot fifty-nine once on the LPGA Tour. Controversy surrounded her the moment she announced her intention to play. Some tour players were for her, and some were adamantly against her playing in a men's event on the PGA Tour. Colonial also took criticism for having the longest-running tour event played at the same course on the PGA Tour, which still holds true today. The tradition of Hogan and the credibility of the Colonial were under scrutiny for allowing this.

A few months before the tournament, I was in Augusta attending the Masters. This just so happened to be the year Martha Burke was protesting the Masters Tournament because they did not have a female member. There were small demonstrations near one of the main gates as you entered Augusta National. As we walked past the demonstration, I noticed that they had buttons with Martha Burke's name and a big slash through her name. Obviously, these people were protesting her as she was protesting a few blocks down from them.

This got me thinking! Annika was going to make history at Colonial, be it good or bad, and we needed something to give her a boost of support. When I came back to Fort Worth, I asked my boss, Dow Finsterwald Jr., if the assistant golf pros could have a button created and sold in the golf shop. Dow said he would be happy for us to create a button to support her. I wanted to cover my bases, so I called the general manager, the tournament director, and Annika's agent. Everyone thought it was a good idea.

Next came the part of what the button should say. I thought about "Annika's Army" and a few other slogans, but I kept coming back to "Go Annika." I thought this signified our support the best.

Then came choosing the color. Initially, pink sounded like a good idea, but I didn't want only women wearing the buttons and thought this would detract from men buying them. I decided on lime green. The color stood out and would be purchased by both men and women. My idea was good, but my ambition wasn't as high as it should've been. The first order was for two thousand buttons, which arrived a few weeks before the tournament. It didn't take long to realize I should have ordered one hundred thousand! We sold out to members and staff before the tournament even began. We ordered as many as we could get for tournament week.

On Pro-Am Monday, the PGA Tour players started coming in the shop and purchasing buttons to wear in support of Annika. Then the media took notice, and every news station and newspaper around the world was showing the lime green "Go Annika" button. This button suddenly became the hottest item around the world for a brief moment. EBay had them listed for fifty-six dollars a button. I couldn't believe it!

Annika didn't make the cut but went on to win the hearts of golfers and nongolfers around the world. Gary Player called the golf shop from South Africa, praising the Colonial and saying he couldn't leave his television from being so excited, watching Annika.

After a whirlwind week for Annika and the Colonial Country Club, we made history. What some people thought was a horrible idea (to let her play) turned out to be historic. Today, the "Go Annika" button sits in the World Golf Hall of Fame. Annika won the hearts of the world with her courageous effort to compete against the men in a PGA Tour event. She said she would only do it once, and it was the greatest week of her life. It was a week I'll never forget and am so thankful I was a small part of golf history.

Thank you, Annika, and thank you, Martha Burke, for the "Go Annika" button idea!

GPS

THE WORLD HAS become so technical with our smartphones that we have become a nation that can't function for a day if we don't have them. Now, I'm as guilty as all of you reading this. I don't know my kids' phone numbers because they are programed into my phone. I don't have to look for directions anywhere because you can ask your phone to get you there and it will.

Recently, I was in Dallas and driving to a hotel that was mapped into my phone. After I checked into the hotel, I was meeting friends for dinner at a restaurant within walking distance of my hotel. I walked out of the hotel lobby and asked my smartphone how to get there. Immediately, the GPS pulled up my location and led me to the restaurant four blocks away.

This got me thinking about mapping out golf courses. I know there are all kinds of devices to give you exact yardage on every hole. All of my caddies have range finders they use to give exact yardage to our members. It makes their jobs more efficient and speeds up the round.

Now, think for a moment about mapping out a golf course for the first time, but you have no GPS unit in your cart and no range finder, only a pin sheet and the yardage markers on the course. Now, let's imagine you have none of this equipment and you get to caddy for Arnold Palmer. You would look over every detail of the golf course so you could tell Mr. Palmer exactly where you need to go and how far it is to each destination. You would also pay attention to certain trees or bunkers on the course that might affect his round. You would pay attention to the green complex and how the grain of the grass might affect a putt. You would pay a lot more attention to details!

If you are a tournament player and you want to elevate your game to another level, pay more attention to the fine details when you play a practice round. I ask my students before they leave for a practice round to be ready for a call from me at any time that evening. They need to be prepared to tell me how they would play any hole I ask them about. I also like to throw in a different wind direction just to throw them off. If they can tell me how they would play each hole, then they are prepared to play the tournament.

GPS devices and smartphones have changed all of our lives for the better! Go play a practice round without technology and see how you perform. Pay attention to the details on the course. Pay attention to wind direction. Pay attention to the sand texture and grain in the greens. Become your own GPS unit for one day and see if it changes the way you see the golf course. After you have done this, I bet you play some of the holes differently than before. If you are a tournament player, you will score better. After you've done this, go back to using your range finder or GPS units, and enjoy the technology you have!

P.S. If you don't have a range finder, we sell them at Whispering Pines!

Guitars Going Out of Tune

MY GUITAR COLLECTION is very dear to my heart. It's so much fun to pull a guitar out of the case and plug it into a powerful amp. One of the things I've never understood is the longer a guitar is not played, the more out of tune it becomes. All guitars have to be tuned at some point, whether they are played or not played. It has never made sense to me if the guitar was perfectly in tune when it was returned to its case, why it would be out of tune a month later. Shouldn't the guitar be in the same tune when it is plugged into a Marshall amp as it was when it was put in the case? Humidity and different temperature changes seem to affect the strings and the wood. That is my conclusion and what the research has shown, but it still doesn't make sense.

Golf swings get out of tune just like guitar strings. When you put away your game for a month and come back, you will most likely be out of tune. It doesn't matter how well you were striking the ball before your game took some time off; seldom do you come back as the same golfer the first time back. Many PGA Tour players take time off after a win and return a few weeks later, but never seem to get their winning form back. This year, Dustin Johnston was winning everything early in the year and hasn't come close to winning over the past few months after returning. Everyone needs a break, especially PGA Tour players, who are on the road and away from their families for weeks, but there are no guarantees they will have the same winning form.

The weekend golfer doesn't get to play or practice every day like professionals, and their games will certainly go out of tune faster, but it's still all relative. PGA guys finishing in the top ten every week and then taking time off and returning missing cuts is the same as the weekend golfer who normally shoots in the low eighties and comes back after a few busy months in the office and shoots in the nineties the first time back.

We all go in and out of tune with our golf games just like guitar strings. The next time you take some time off, start back with a tune-up from your golf professional. With a little work on the range, you can get your swing back in tune in no time!

Higher Expectations

If you try and hit it close and you don't, you're probably not going to be close.

If you try and hole the shot and don't, you're probably going to be close.

If you try and make par and don't, you will probably make bogey or higher.

If you try and make birdie and don't, you will probably make par.

The next round you play, have a higher expectation on every shot!

Hit the Delete Button

Many of us hit a poor shot and beat ourselves up and then proceed to hit the next shot poorly. There's nothing wrong with being upset or even mad about hitting a bad shot, but you have to let it go before your next shot. Allow yourself to process a poor shot as you ride to your ball. Once you get out of the cart, hit the delete button in your mind and start fresh. If you have emotion left over from your previous shot, your odds of hitting the next shot well will decrease. When you receive junk email, you automatically delete it and move on to the next email. Delete and hit refresh the next time you set up for your shot after hitting your last shot poorly, and you will have more success on the links!

Hotel California

BLOCK PRACTICE IS taking new information and applying it specifically to your practice session. For example, you take a lesson, and your instructor asks you to work on one specific move to rotate your hips to start your downswing. No new information will be given by your instructor until this move is incorporated into your swing. Block practice requires hours of work to make a new swing adjustment become second nature.

One of my passions is playing the guitar, and it's very common to learn sections of a song before putting it all together. "Hotel California" is a song that comes to mind that took me hours to perfect specific notes. Once the intro of the song was mastered, the next section of notes could be worked on and perfected. The beauty of music is hearing it all come together after learning all the pieces and letting the music flow through your hands and into the instrument.

Random practice is taking numerous pieces of your practice routine and spending short amounts of time on each section. For example, work twenty minutes on chipping, twenty minutes on putting, and twenty minutes on your bunker game to round out an hour of short-game practice. This would be like playing "Hotel California," "Life in the Fast Lane," and "Tequila Sunrise" one after the other in their entirety. The only way to play those songs consecutively is by spending block practice time learning them. Once they are learned, you can play the concert.

Studies have shown random practice to be much more effective than block practice once a skill is learned. Some of my students need work on specific areas and need to spend time in a block practice setting, but once the skill is learned, they move into random practice.

The next time you are with your instructor and he works on one specific move in your swing, spend the appropriate amount of time to incorporate the change. If the intro to "Hotel California" was never learned, it would have been impossible for me to play the entire song.

Once you've mastered the new swing change, you can then add the next piece. The next time this song comes on the radio, remember it takes a lot of time and practice to play this iconic song. The Eagles perfected it and never think about how their fingers are moving along the strings. When you spend the appropriate amount of time on the swing changes your instructor wants you to make, your swing will flow like being "on a dark desert highway" with cool wind in your hair.

How Danny Willet Paid for
the Family Vacation

In 2007, Danny Willet played for England in the Spirit International at Whispering Pines. He was a young English kid who hit the ball a mile and could make a ton of birdies every round. A few months after the tournament, one of our members (originally from England) called and made a tee time. The member told me he was bringing out Danny Willet and his girlfriend at the time, who played for the University of Texas.

When the day arrived, Danny walked in speaking with his strong English accent and blasting his driver over our first tee building at the end of our driving range. It wasn't my intention to play that day, but my member asked me to join the three of them. We were not very busy, and it seemed like it would be fun to play with a former Spirit participant, so my clubs were thrown on my cart, and off to the first tee we went.

When you are playing with a kid who is going to turn pro and probably be very successful, it becomes hard to find a fair gambling game. My member decided the only fair match would be Danny against the three of us. To make it more fun, we played a scramble format from the member tees and Danny played his own ball from the Spirit tees.

Danny hit the ball extremely well and had all the shots around the greens. When we arrived at the 9th hole, we had all finished with the same amount of strokes. The best we could do was tie Danny with the three of us playing scramble!

Since that day, I've paid attention to his career and watched how he's become one of the best players in Europe. It was mentioned by me numerous times to our members that this kid would win at Augusta someday. Watching his performance at the start of the 2016 season, my prediction seemed to be more valid. Gambling isn't in my nature, but it's fun to place one bet in Vegas every year on a Dallas Cowboys game.

This got me asking some of my friends who frequent Las Vegas what the line on Danny Willet winning the Masters would pay. The line was 125 to 1 six weeks before the Masters and moved to 65 to 1 after Danny played another great event a few weeks before the Masters. This was a Ben Crenshaw moment. I had a feeling!

Like previously mentioned, I'm not a big bettor, but decided to place a fifty-dollar bet on Mr. Willet to win at Augusta. Everyone around the club had heard me talk about this for months, so it was time to put my money where my mouth was and hope for the best.

Jordan Spieth was the favorite and is a former Spirit alumni, as well. I am a huge Spieth fan and cheer for him every time he has a chance to win. Everything in me wanted Jordan to win the Masters! You couldn't help rooting for the kid from Dallas as he made his way to Amen Corner with a five-shot lead. My fifty-dollar bet didn't even matter anymore, because Jordan was about to make history. Then the unthinkable happened on the 12th hole: Jordan hit two balls in the water and relinquished the lead he had held since Thursday. It made me sick to watch what transpired on that 150-yard hole.

As Danny continued to hit great shots and make birdies, my focus turned toward my bet. Suddenly, there was a chance Danny might win and my prediction would come to fruition. As we all saw it play out on that incredible Sunday, the eventual winner was Danny Willet from Yorkshire, England. My prediction had come true, and my bet paid 65 to 1! It was actually hard to believe everything that happened during the final round. Members immediately started texting me with congratulations, asking who was going to win the US Open. It was an amazingly lucky bet, and the payout will pay for me and my boys to go to Destin this summer.

Danny Willet, thank you for playing an incredible tournament and making me look smart. As for my prediction for the US Open, I'm cheering for Jordan Spieth. He is a class act and has made golf a better game!

How Much Do You Love Your Kids?

THIS IS A silly question because we love every one of our children exactly the same. Most people have a favorite club in their bag, but the truth is the ball has no idea what club you are swinging. Love every club in your bag just like you love each one of your children.

Humility, Yips, and
the US Open Qualifier

A FEW MONTHS ago, I told my oldest son I was thinking about trying to qualify for the US Open, and I wanted him to caddy for me. I'm a golf professional, not a professional golfer, but love the game and thought why not give it a try!

Before I could change my mind, my son had posted on Facebook that I was qualifying for the Open. I'm not a Facebook guy and had no idea the response I would get the next day from teachers at his school, my parents, and anyone else I seemed to come in contact with who had read his Facebook page. Most people thought I would be *playing* in the Open and had no idea what goes in to trying to *qualify*. When people mentioned the US Open, I would tell them I was trying out for *American Idol* next week! It was actually comical how people reacted to my mythical quest. It felt like *Tin Cup* in many ways, and I was Roy McElroy trying to impress my son, rather than the "Doctor Lady," as Cheech would say.

As a golf professional, I run the golf operation at Whispering Pines. My job has many responsibilities just like all golf professionals in the world. I teach, run tournaments, manage a large staff of caddies and supervisors, play golf with the membership, run a golf shop … and the list goes on. Basically, my job is to make sure everyone who visits Whispering Pines has a world-class golf experience. Nowhere in my job description does it say qualify for the US Open, but how could I pull out now? My son was so proud, and the closer the qualifier came, the more people started finding out.

The negative to all of this was my son couldn't miss school and would not be able to caddy. This was a real bummer because I really wanted this to be a father-son day on the links. The pressure was building, and

I thought maybe I should hit some balls and at least practice a little bit. We had hosted the Big 12 Championship a few weeks before and then had a busy week at the club, so practice had been limited, but I did start getting out and playing a bit more than normal. My ball striking was good, and everything seemed to be coming together in my game. This was actually exciting because I only play a few tournaments a year and I can usually predict my rounds within a few strokes, and they are never going to be real low.

When I first got into the golf business twenty years ago, I played in section events and loved teeing it up any chance I got to play. In college, we qualified or played a tournament almost every week, so tournament golf was just business as usual. As time has gone by and the tournaments have become less and less, anxiety and dread started to creep into my game. If a tournament was on my schedule, the closer it came, the more anxiety I started to feel about posting a score. The past few years, it has gotten much better, and I have actually played some decent tournament rounds. The crazy thing about all of this is none of this happens if I'm playing with members or friends or even betting in friendly games on the course. It amazes me what has happened to some of the best players like Ian Baker Finch, David Duval, or even Craig Perks after winning the Players Championship, but I can relate …

Well, let's get back to the Open Qualifier. My first assistant and I traveled to the tournament site and played our practice rounds. It was actually fun, and I felt like I was back in college preparing for a tournament. We played the course as far back as you could play it and hit all types of shots around the green in preparation for the upcoming event. When we finished our practice round, I realized the course fit my eye really well, and I figured that if keeping score, I had shot around 76 or 77. As little as I play, I was actually okay with four or five over par. My main reason for trying to qualify was my son and the fun of what if I got all going for one round!

Tournament day had arrived, and my second assistant was caddying for me since my son had to be in school. I was unusually calm for a tournament round and actually was very focused. The USGA official called my name to the tee, and I started my routine. It wasn't a great tee shot, but we were off and running for a chance at Olympic Club. I hit a very solid hybrid on the long par-five for my second shot and ripped a four iron right at the pin, coming up just short of the green. I had hit two solid shots, and the nerves were in check, but my chip wasn't very good, and two putts later I made bogey.

The next hole was a drivable par-four, but I had made up my mind that the three wood and then the nine iron was my best route to play this dangerous hole. I made a mistake teeing the ball too low and came out of my posture hitting the ball thin and in the water. After teeing up again, I hit a good shot along with a good nine iron, but proceeded to three putts. The next hole was another sloppy bogey!

Now, the turning point to the round: I smashed a drive on my fourth hole and had 165 yards into the green. My assistant and I agreed the seven iron was the perfect club. The ball rocketed off the clubface, stopping twenty feet from the pin. At that point, I realized I wasn't going to have the round of my life, but those two shots gave me confidence that the game was turning around. My caddie and I studied the extremely slick side hill, downhill, down grain, and putt. I breathed on this putt and watched it pick up pace. I watched in disbelief as it rolled ten feet past the cup. The comeback putt for par slid three feet past the cup, and then I proceeded to miss that putt with a power lip out that rolled four feet down the hill. Without taking any time, I addressed the putt and missed that one. I tapped the putt into the hole and walked away in total disbelief! I had to ask my caddie what my score was because I honestly did not know.

The rest of the round was like playing in a fog, and then I started yipping numerous short putts on the perfect but extremely fast greens. I fought as hard as I could and played some solid holes on my back nine but just couldn't get anything out of my game. Embarrassment started to set in, and I knew I was about to post one of my highest scores in the past twenty years. Oh yeah, and that Facebook thing, the teachers, my parents, and everyone who had some crazy idea that a golf professional who averages 77 most days was going to qualify for the US Open.

John Peterson shot 63 that day, and my very best round of my life is still three shots higher than his score. It wasn't going to happen, but I never saw it happening like it did. When I came home, I was so bummed out! My passion is teaching, and I love getting players to reach their potential. I had students playing in this tournament who I had coached for this specific event, but I couldn't get my personal game to the level I had hoped for.

When I got home, the family was supportive, and my son was told to stay off Facebook. I put my two young boys to bed that evening as my oldest son and wife went to Target to buy a few things. When they got back, my son handed me a card. The title was "I Believe," and it touched me more than shooting a 63 at the qualifier. My wife had written on the inside a note of encouragement and what an inspiration I am to my boys, and my oldest son had written, "It's just an up and down! I've had many! Love, Dylan."

When you put it all into perspective, my score could never compare to the love and support my family gives me. Yes, I shot one heck of a bad round! Yes, I tried as hard as I could on every shot! Yes, I wanted to "no card," but what example would that have been to my kids? Who knows, I might try something crazy like this again someday, but this year on Father's Day, I will be at home with my family watching the US Open with the ones I love.

I-45

I CAN'T BEGIN to count the number of times I've been on the driving range and asked a student what target they were trying to hit and they invariably were twenty yards off line. Words of wisdom I've always mentioned when I see this issue: "Would you point your car north on I-45 from Huntsville to get to Houston?" They always look at me curiously and say, "Of course not." I ask how they plan on getting to the target if their body is lined toward Dallas and they are trying to go to Houston. You have to make some major adjustments to get there if you are going to eventually arrive at your intended destination.

When your alignment is off and you make a good swing, your ball will go where you are aligned. If you have bad alignment, you have to make an adjustment in order to hit the ball where you want the ball to end up. Basically, if your alignment is bad, you have to make a bad swing to get the ball to your target!

Good alignment follows a simple routine of lining your clubface toward the target and lining your body parallel to the club. Once the club is aligned to your target, you don't need to look at the target again, only adjust your body to the club. Most people look at the target and start adjusting their club and body while continuing to look at their target. I've seen people do this so many times, and they actually think they are perfectly aligned. The problem is their eyes have never left the target regardless of how far their body has moved in the wrong direction.

Greg Norman was one of the best drivers of the golf ball in the history of the game. He always aligned his club first and then his body. Try this the next time you play a round and see if it doesn't make a difference.

If You Already Knew the Outcome

How many times have you recorded a show or a sporting event with plans to watch later and then found out the outcome before you were able to watch? If you recorded a Dallas Cowboys game and then found out they won the game, or recorded a reality show and then found out who got voted off before you had a chance to watch it, you wouldn't you watch the program differently. When you know the outcome, you don't care if your team is ten points behind with five minutes left, because you know they will pull it out and win. When you know the villain of your favorite reality show gets voted off, you can sit back with no worries, knowing they get will voted off.

What if you saw your golf game as a prerecorded event, and you knew the score you had already posted? Think about it! If you saw yourself winning your club championship before you played the club championship, you would play relaxed and know your score was going to be great. I often tell the junior golfers I work with to play as many holes in their mind while falling asleep in bed every evening as they can. If you have already seen yourself hitting a great drive on the first hole or making birdies, your body will react to what it has imagined.

Great players think like this! They have already seen themselves holding the trophy at the end of the tournament. The next time you have an important tournament, start getting your mind ready for greatness. When you play a hole in your mind, you should always make birdie. You can imagine anything you want, so why not imagine perfection around the course? The greatest discovery in psychology is that people become what they think. Get rid of the stinkin' thinkin' in your game! Set the DVR and record your next round of golf before you play it, and expect a great outcome!

Investing for the Future

———— ✦ ————

OVER THE PAST twenty years, I've invested in my 401K at all the clubs I've worked for. They've all matched a percentage of my contributions, and it's been amazing how the money adds up when you invest consistently over time. There have also been some really dumb investments made over the years on my behalf in the stock market. Someone tells me about a great company or my impulsiveness to make a quick dollar gets the best of me. Every single time, the stock purchased for the quick turnaround investment has never worked out for me.

This made me think about how often students come to me with the quick-fix tip they heard on the Golf Channel or read in a magazine. The infomercial that promises you lower scores or the wedge that makes it impossible to miss hit rarely produce the miracle they claim. All of these are like my investments in companies I knew very little about and lost money to.

There isn't a quick fix to your golf game! You should invest in your game consistently over the long term with a knowledgeable instructor. The students who've worked with me for years tend to hear a lot of the same lessons from me. The challenges in your swing today were there five years ago and will be there five years from now if you continue to chase the quick fix. Consistent swing maintenance is the key for all of you reading this.

There was a young man who lived near Amarillo and used to take lessons from me at Colonial. I'm not sure of the actual mileage, but it was a long way to drive for a golf lesson. Before this young man arrived in Fort Worth, I already knew exactly what would be communicated for the hour we would spend together. He made the same slide move with the club coming over his plane line. Every lesson, he was told the exact same thing, and within five minutes, he always hit the ball beautifully. The next fifty-five minutes would be spent monitoring and making sure he was consistently rotating and allowing the club to stay on plane. This young man would have new ideas about his swing every time he showed up and always seemed dumbfounded that the correction was the same for every lesson.

The truth is, most lessons given to my students at Whispering Pines tend to be consistent information they've heard before. Unfortunately, most students hear the latest "stock tip" for their swing and go invest in the wrong thing.

Butch Harmon instructed Tiger Woods for years, and they had tremendous success. Tiger was quoted as saying he left Butch because he wasn't learning anything new. Sometimes, searching for some new technique in your swing is like changing your investment strategy because you don't think your returns are good enough. Over the long term, Tiger Woods played incredibly well under the instruction of Butch Harmon and had one of the best swings on tour. He has had three instructors since Butch and isn't the same player he used to be. In fairness, he has had injuries and personal issues, but wouldn't it have been interesting to see what he might have accomplished if he would have stayed consistent with his investment in his swing?

Think of your golf swing as an investment. Get with your instructor and identify the consistent flaws needing repair, then make the changes needed to produce consistent results. Invest in those swing changes for the long term and watch your investment grow every round!

Doesn't Matter How It Happened as Long as It Worked Out

FROM TIME TO time, my girlfriend has a tendency to forget her purse. When we first started dating, she left it at the Subway restaurant in Trinity, and fortunately, it was kept by the manager until we came back. She is a smart, intelligent, beautiful woman who is not absentminded or forgetful, but the purse thing is her bugaboo.

Yesterday, we were in San Francisco and arrived at the airport to catch our flight back to Houston after an incredible four days on the West Coast. When we pulled our luggage into the terminal, she realized her purse was in the rental car three miles away. She immediately became very worried that someone might steal her purse. We made a call to the rental car company, and the lady who answered the phone could not have been nicer. She told us she had the purse in her possession and offered to personally drive to our terminal and meet me. This was some of the best customer service I've ever seen! My girlfriend was still distraught that she had forgotten her purse, even though we were getting it back. I told her it wasn't a big deal and we all forget things at times. Within ten minutes, her purse arrived with all of its content intact. As we walked to the ticket counter to check our luggage, I laughed and told her it didn't matter what happened as long as it all worked out. As soon as I made the statement, I said, "That's the title of my next article."

How many times do we play a hole and butcher it from tee to green, yet somehow still make par? We can leave the green and beat ourselves up all the way to the next hole, but the scorecard still says we made par. It doesn't matter if you drove your golf ball in the woods; if you walk away with par, then it all worked out.

We all make mistakes in life and on the golf course, but it doesn't matter—if it all works out! The next time you're having that kind of hole, remember this story and laugh all the way to the next tee box after you write down par.

(If you happen to see my girlfriend's purse on the back of a chair in a restaurant, please give me a call at Whispering Pines so I can return it!)

It's All the Way You Play It

PEBBLE BEACH HOSTS the Mizuno Pro-Am every year the week after the AT&T Pro-Am. For fourteen years, my staff program was through Mizuno, so we always received an invitation to this fun event. The Pro-Am limited players' handicaps to be no higher than twenty-two. This is understandable, because the courses are difficult and you want players to be able to get around the course in a reasonable amount of time.

One thing I've always tried to do as a golf professional is to take different members on trips. It is important to me that my members get to experience the Pine Valleys or Cypress Points of the world, along with Pro-Am events. One day playing in the Friday Junior Game at Colonial Country Club, Bobby Patton asked me if he could go to the Mizuno Pro-Am. The maximum handicap came to mind immediately because Bobby's handicap was a thirty-eight at the time. It was brought up how difficult the courses play and how many balls could be lost in this event. Without missing a beat, Bobby said, "My golf bag has plenty of balls." At that moment, there was no turning back, and Bobby Patton would be playing in his first Mizuno Pro-Am.

Bobby started taking lessons from me twenty-three years ago when I was an assistant at Colonial. When we played a wolf game, he would always get two shots on the par-three 4th hole. If he hit a decent shot, he was going to pig whoever picked him and play the hole without a partner, usually always taking our money. We also always had a standard five-dollar side bet, where he received one and a half shots per hole playing match-play format. This was a great way for a broke assistant to make some extra cash—until the lessons started to take effect.

One day, standing on the 18th tee, the broke assistant was way down in the match. Bobby has always been generous and would give you a way out if you wanted to make another bet. Bobby walked over to my bag and said he could use a new two iron. The broke assistant smiled and said, "It's a bet." Mr. Patton still has that two iron somewhere in his house!

Okay, back to the Mizuno Pro-Am. The excitement of playing Pebble Beach is always one of the highlights of my year. It never gets old walking along the cliffs and marveling at the beauty of the Monterrey Peninsula. We reached the famous 8th hole at Pebble, and Bobby asked me where he was supposed to hit the tee shot. The aiming rock is about one hundred yards from the tee, and he was told to hit right over it with a slight draw. The ball screamed low and left, which was the typical shot back then, leaving him with another blind shot up the cliff. He asked where to play the next shot, and after receiving the information, he fired an iron to the top of the cliff.

If you've never had the experience of standing on top of the cliff of the 8th hole at Pebble Beach, you need to put it on your bucket list. It is truly one of the most spectacular views in all of golf. The shot requires a 175-yard carry over the Pacific Ocean to a very small green. Jack Nicklaus said it's the greatest second shot in golf. Unfortunately, this was going to be Bobby's *third* shot.

As we walked to the ball, he asked where to hit his third shot. I'll never forget the look on his face when I pointed to the green! He looked at me and said, "There is no way!" With a huge grin on my face, he was advised to hit his third shot back toward the sixth hole. At this point, it was time for me to play my shot and drive the cart to the green. Bobby said he would walk the rest of the hole and meet me at the green. The rest of the team was trying to figure out what Bobby was doing, as they had already reached the green and were waiting. As my cart neared the green, I looked back to see Bobby waggling the club and then making a beautiful golf swing for a thirty-eight handicap. The ball sailed through the air and landed on the top left corner of the green and started to roll toward the hole. To all of our amazement, the ball continued to roll toward hole, kissing the flag stick and dropping to the bottom of the cup for a crowd-pleasing par.

Bobby threw his club up in the air, and we all cheered from the green. As he walked down the cliff and approached the green, he smiled and said, "It's all the way you play it." We have laughed about that moment for years and continue to use that line when we play rounds together at Whispering Pines.

Bobby Patton was a Fort Worth lawyer at the time, playing to a thirty-eight handicap. Today, he is one of the owners of the LA Dodgers and plays to an eighteen handicap. He has worked very hard on his game over the years and has lowered his handicap more than any of my students. He even shot 79 a few years ago at Pebble Beach in Pat Green's tournament. Bobby is one of my best friends and still the same guy today he was twenty-three years ago playing in the Friday Junior Game. Proud of you, Big Bank!

Lamborghinis, BMWs, and Fords

IN THE PAST two days, I've been asked about driver distance from more than one student. Everyone wants to hit the ball farther, and every week on the PGA Tour, we all see the guys bombing drives 300 plus.

When I worked at Colonial Country Club, it was always fun to go out the Sunday before tournament week and test the game. The golf course played so much more difficult than the normal conditions the other fifty-one weeks of the year. The rough was so thick, and the greens were so firm and fast, making the course play from four to five shots harder than the normal member round. One thing that was easier about tournament conditions was the speed of the fairways. If the superintendent were to stimp the fairways during the tour event,

I would bet they were rolling at least 10.5, which is faster than most greens speeds at your home course.

When a PGA Tour player hits a drive, the balls run out much more than your home course fairways. This doesn't mean these guys don't hit the ball a country mile, but it's not completely apples to apples. Everyone should use the data available through FlightScope or TrackMan to make the necessary adjustments to their equipment to maximize distance, but there is only so much distance you can gain through technology. Working out and staying flexible are other ways to create speed in your swing, as well. Once you've done all of the things mentioned to create the longest possible shots with the best ball flights, your work is done.

We had a member last week let me drive his brand-new Lamborghini. I've never in my life felt this type of power in a car, and my BMW certainly could never keep up with his Lamborghini. I could make all the adjustments possible to my car, but it wasn't made to go 200 mph. My point of this car analogy is that Dustin Johnson is built like a Lamborghini, and I'm built like a 3 Series BMW, and some of you are built like a Ford truck. All three of the vehicles can get to the intended destination, but they all get there in a different way. Luke Donald doesn't hit the ball very far compared to the rest of the guys on tour, and yet he reached the number one ranking in the world by having a phenomenal short game. Dustin Johnson reached number one in the world with massive distance. They both reached number one in world golf rankings, and both had different strengths.

Do what you can to create more distance, and then focus on the other parts of your game. Many times, we get so focused on the distance we have that other parts of our game suffer. Have a balanced approach to your game and don't neglect any part of it chasing one particular thing. Your scorecard doesn't have any place on it that asks how far you hit your drive!

Limo Ride

EVERY YEAR, THE majority of the golf world heads to Orlando, Florida, for the PGA Merchandise Show. The week is golf overload in every form and fashion, but it's a week we all look forward to. The PGA Show is wonderful for educational opportunities, buying merchandise, trying out all the new golf clubs, and socializing with old friends.

One of my members is a member at a club in West Palm, and he thought we should play golf for a few days after the PGA Show. He arranged a transportation service to pick me up at my hotel and drive to his home at the Floridian so I wouldn't have to rent a car. The driver showed up right on time at my hotel, and with a short introduction, we loaded up my clubs and luggage and headed south. As we were driving for a good twenty minutes, I noticed we were still in Orlando. The driver seemed to be confused and wasn't sure of his directions. About thirty minutes had gone by, and we were back in the convention center area, where I had been the past three days. At this point, it was necessary to ask the driver if he knew how to get to West Palm. He was very flustered and said he had missed his turn and couldn't figure out how to get on the correct highway. Bewildered and aggravated, I asked him to put directions into his GPS to get us on the right track. He apologized and said his GPS had quit working the previous week. I then asked him to put the address in his IPhone, and he again apologized and said he didn't have an IPhone, but had been thinking about getting one.

"You are telling me I got the only driver in Florida that doesn't have a GPS unit or an IPhone?"

He apologized once more, and I told him it was joke and laughed while pulling out my IPhone to input the address. Before long, we were headed south to the Floridian and talked about numerous topics for the next two hours. When we arrived, he apologized over and over for getting us lost. I told him it wasn't a big deal. We arrived safe and proceeded to head to the front door of the house.

My driver wasn't prepared for the trip and the lack of preparation made for an entertaining trip (to say the least). A round of golf can be much like my driver planning the trip to West Palm Beach: If you're not prepared, you could have numerous roadblocks and wrong turns. Preparation for a round of golf should take the same consideration as a good transportation service would take with their clients. The car should have a full tank of gas, the trip details should be entered into a GPS, there should be a few bottled waters for the client, and the trip should be a success.

The next time you are planning for your Saturday round or upcoming tournament, go through your checklist. Make sure your body is fueled up and hydrated, and go through your yardage book to map out your round. If you do these things, you will be more successful on the golf course and hopefully not make any wrong turns like we did on our trip to West Palm.

The Medicine Ball Throw for the Perfect Impact Position

Backswing: The weight of the medicine ball should make your hands feel like they are dropping into the impact position!

Impact: This should feel like throwing a medicine ball in a downward direction.

After Impact: The medicine ball should be thrown a few feet in front of your intended impact position. Your arms and club should create a Y position after you've hit the ball.

Mr. 58

WE ALL ADMIRE Jason Day's and Rory McIlory's swings. The grace and technical perfection they have makes every golfer want to swing the way they do. I'm going on the record by saying that there has never been a golf instructor teach one of their students to swing like Jim Furyk! In the words of *Tin Cup*, "My swing feels like an unfolding lawn chair" comes to mind when we think of Mr. Furyk's swing. Well, this golf swing, as quirky as it looks, produced the lowest golf score ever in a PGA Tour event.

Every week, instructors work with students trying to create perfect techniques. Perfection is unattainable in this game. Byron Nelson said, "Find a swing you can repeat and spend the rest of your life working on it." What great advice to all the golfers out there working on a *beautiful* swing, rather than a *productive* swing. Miller Barber, Raymond Floyd, John Daly, and the great Arnold Palmer all won majors with unorthodox positions. So why do we try so hard to make our swings look like Louis Oosthuizen or Adam Scott? The same reason beauty products are a billion-dollar industry: We all want to look good! Would you rather shoot lower scores or look good and shoot higher scores? At the end of the day, the only thing that matters is your score.

Jim Furyk absolutely drives me nuts with his mannerisms over each shot, but there is no denying this golfer figured it out and didn't care what anyone thought. Can you imagine how many smirks he received in his junior golf days? All those kids with great positions and technique probably haven't won a US Open, and they for sure haven't shot 58 in a PGA Tour event.

The purpose of this story is that the most unusual swing on the PGA Tour shot the lowest score ever! Work with your instructor in areas where you can improve your scores, and quit worrying about the perfect golf swing. Jim Furyk will be in the Golf Hall of Fame someday, and you will be a better player when you find your repeatable swing—regardless of how it looks.

Never Judge a Book Before
You've Read It

ONE OF THE great pleasures of working in the golf business is teaching the game. Sam Houston State University is located in the town I live in, and they have a Professional Golf Management Program. The PGM Program allows young men and women to get a business degree and their PGA Class A card. The kids go through an educational process to prepare them for a job in the golf industry. These kids learn about turf grass, golf cart fleet management, the rules of golf, running tournaments, merchandising a golf shop, and teaching the game, along with numerous other things.

One of the requirements of being a PGA professional and graduating this program is to pass a playability test. The kids have to play thirty-six holes and score under a certain number based on the difficulty of the course. I'm blessed to be part of this program through teaching. Every student who has not passed their PAT has to come see me for two hours of instruction every semester until they pass. I thoroughly enjoy working with these kids because we have a common goal—and that's passing the PAT.

Along with working with them to make them better players, I also have the opportunity to mentor these kids. They all have questions about the golf business and how to excel in the industry. I don't have all the answers, but I have had a lot of wonderful moments on the range talking through challenges in business and in life with these young adults. When the freshmen arrive, I can usually tell who will be successful and who might struggle.

One day, a guy came in with a lot of tattoos and didn't fit the typical stereotype of a golfer. We worked on his game, and I knew pretty quickly he was going to need a lot of work. We all like to think we are not judgmental, but I felt myself feeling this way because of all the tattoos. I noticed one of his tattoos was a specific date and asked him what had happened on that date. He told me that was the day where his unit came under fire in Afghanistan and he lost a number of friends. I immediately felt horrible for judging someone I didn't know based on some tattoos. This guy fought for my freedom and kept the greatest country in world safe.

From that moment on, he was my most important student. I wanted this guy to pass his PAT more than any student I've ever instructed. He came and took lessons from me for a few years and finally passed his PAT. When he called me to tell me, it was the happiest I've ever been for one of my PGM players. He put in a lot of hard work and practiced until he accomplished his goal. I apologized to him about judging him and told him to mention to every employer he works for about the meaning of the tattoos. I learned a great lesson that day and will always remember to open the book before I judge the cover. Thank you, Brooks Muse, for fighting for this country and helping me see an ugly flaw in myself.

No Stinkin' Thinkin'

I'VE NEVER MET anybody who said they were a great putter who wasn't. I've never met anyone who said they were a bad putter who wasn't a bad putter. The way you think about your game becomes a self-fulfilling prophecy. Think and say only positive things about your game, and you will change the way you play.

The One-Ball Rule

THE ONE-BALL RULE in golf means you have to play with the same type and brand of golf ball you started the round with. Under this rule, you are not allowed to tee off with a Titleist NXT and switch to a Pro V1 when you reach the green to putt. I remember playing in scrambles as a kid and hitting Top Flites off the tee and putting with the old Tour Balata golf ball. This was great because the Top Flite went farther and the Balata was soft to putt with.

As I write this, I'm on a flight to Arizona to tee it up for a few days at Whisper Rock Golf Club. Desert golf isn't my favorite, mainly because I have trouble with my tee ball and tend to hit shots into the desert. I'm a work in progress and getting better, but always challenged on these types of courses.

So what if I get to the first tee and put only one ball in my bag? Do you think I would focus better? Do you think I would weigh the risk of certain shots over water? What about going for the green on the par-five with out of bounds near green? The answer is yes, I would definitely change my strategy and the way I play the golf course.

When Tiger Woods was leading the US Open at Pebble Beach, he hit a ball in the ocean on the 18th hole. He asked his caddy for another ball but had no idea this was the only ball left in his bag. His caddie knew this and asked Tiger to hit a different club to ensure he put the ball in play. Tiger disagreed and ripped driver down the fairway and went on to win the US Open the next day. Fast forward a month later, and Tiger Woods is playing in the British Open. He and his caddy have a discussion about what club he should hit, with Tiger disagreeing again. As they walked down the fairway, Tiger asked his caddy why he had wanted Tiger to hit another club the previous month at the US Open after he had hit his ball in the ocean. His caddy then admitted he had only had one ball left in his bag that day because he had given a couple of balls away before the round and the bag hadn't been restocked before they teed off.

This would have been one of the biggest caddy disasters ever if Tiger had hit that second ball in the water, but he didn't and won by a record margin.

Now, here is your one-ball challenge! The next round of golf you play, only bring one ball to the first tee. See how your mindset changes, knowing you only have one ball. If you can finish the round with only one golf ball, you've played well and you've taken a strategic approach to each hole. I tried this a few weeks ago and hit an errant tee shot on the twelfth hole, losing my only ball. Having to ask one of your members for a golf ball to finish your round is embarrassing, especially when you are on Titleist's staff and get golf balls for free.

My flight is just about over, and I'll be teeing it up very soon. I'm going to try the one-ball challenge today and hope I don't have to repay my members with a couple of sleeves of golf balls after the round!

Past—Present—Future

TODAY'S SWING FLAW was last year's swing flaw and will be tomorrow's swing flaw if not corrected today. How many lessons have you taken where your golf professional tells you something about your swing that he's told you numerous times in past lessons? Most golf lessons have a lot of repeat information when an instructor sees the student on a limited basis. This is the case when a student doesn't put in the time to change motor skills in his swing. Students who take lessons on a regular basis usually have fewer issues than students who come out once every couple of months for a lesson. The more we repeat a bad motor skill, the more engrained the motor skill becomes.

I'm a huge believer in understanding the swing flaws and putting a plan together to attain better results. The difficulty is the student not working enough on the specific flaw to ever overcome the swing flaw. If you slide your hips on the downswing, rather than rotate them, you can have numerous issues with your ball striking. If you come out of your posture at impact, your ball striking will never be consistent. When your instructor tells you to work on a certain issue in your golf swing, you should spend enough time to get the flaw eliminated, or it will be your same flaw in the future.

Many of you reading this are thinking about how many times you've been told about XYZ in your swing. More than once, I've had a student tell me they've always done XYZ. If you've always done XYZ and never spent time to correct XYZ, you will always have XYZ in your swing.

The next time you take a golf lesson, pay attention to the information your instructor is telling you. If he is saying some of the same things you've been told in the past, then you need to put in the work to correct these flaws in the present. If you correct them today, you're going to be better in the future!

Playing with a Legend

A FEW WEEKS ago, I received an email from one of my members, asking if I would like to play golf with him and a few friends. I agreed and then asked who would be playing with us. He told me Lee Trevino! I immediately blocked my entire day. Lee Trevino is someone I've always wanted to play golf with and ask questions of. I've been a fan since he made his hole-in-one in the skins game at PGA West.

The day arrived, and Lee showed up on the range and started holding court with all of our members. He was just like you would imagine; he never quit talking and had everyone doubled over laughing.

We warmed up on the range, then headed to the first hole. After we all took pictures with Lee, it was time to tee it up. There I am, a kid who grew up in Tishomingo, Oklahoma, playing with a living legend! I was nervous and excited for what the day would hold.

All of us needed a mulligan, but Lee striped his right down the middle as he repeated the entire day. In twenty-seven holes, he missed only two shots that were noticeable. It was the most impressive ball striking I've personally ever witnessed. When we reached the 13th hole, he hit his second shot fat, leaving around fifty yards to the pin for his third. He mentioned he wouldn't need his putter after he hit the shot. I had walked up ahead and was standing next to the green when he hit his forty-seven-year-old Spalding sand wedge with twenty degrees of bounce. You could hear the ball spinning as it hit the green, took one big hop, and stopped two feet away. He looked at all of us and just laughed.

The 14th hole at Whispering Pines has a large pine tree named after President Bush. I had our group play from the Spirit tee on this hole because it is such a spectacular tee shot. Lee commented on the beauty of the hole and then asked where he should play his shot. I went through my golf pro speech, which I've given a hundred times on that hole. Lee listened and then started to work into his stance. He never stopped talking as he set the clubhead behind the ball. He mentioned to us that he was going to hit a fade at the second knot on the President Bush pine. I've been the pro at Whispering Pines for nearly ten years and never noticed a knot, let alone the second knot. The ball ripped off the tee and started five yards left of the tree and then started to fade back at—you guessed it—the second knot. I promise the ball missed the knot by less than a foot and landed in the fairway. We all looked at each other in amazement and then looked at Lee. He once again just smiled and told us that is what he said he was going to do.

The entire day, he told stories about the old players, new players, and the rounds he played with Hogan and Nicklaus. It was mesmerizing to listen to someone who had been there with those legendary players and competed against them. I asked how much he practiced back then, and he told me that during the off-season, he would hit a thousand balls a day, not counting his short game. He would play golf and then find a lighted driving range to go hit more balls. Lee created a repeatable swing by practicing relentlessly, which ultimately made him one of the best ball strikers the game has ever seen.

After the round, we had lunch and then went to the Needler, which is our new par-three course at Whispering Pines. We played a scramble against the other foursome, and for the rest of my life, I can tell my kids I was partners with Lee Trevino.

The sun was beginning to set as we played our twenty-seventh hole of the day. It was a magical day like no other day I've had on the golf course. I've been very blessed to play with numerous celebrities and can honestly say this was the best time I've had on the course with someone famous. Lee was humble, entertaining, and an unbelievably impressive ball striker.

Lee Trevino is a teacher at heart. He helped everyone with their game, and you could tell he enjoyed this immensely. He is a living legend and the game of golf has been blessed to have him!

Practice Session Should Mimic the Course You Will Be Playing

In the late 80s, eight college golfers watched in amazement as Dr. Gil Morgan hit one irons 230 yards into a 30 mph wind, each shot coming off low enough to go under a goalpost with penetrating precision. He told us he would need this shot numerous times in the British Open and would be practicing the shot in the following weeks in preparation. This was a great lesson for all of us college guys hoping to one day play the PGA Tour.

When the Masters is played this spring in Augusta, Georgia, the tour professionals will prepare differently from a normal PGA Tour event. Working the ball from right to left through the tall pines has seemed to be the preferred ball flight of past champions. There has never been a Masters champion who didn't have a phenomenal short game, either. Augusta's green complexes test the best players in the world with every shot imaginable. All the past champions have had great imaginations around the treacherous greens. The list of Seve Ballesteros, Jordan Spieth, Phil Mickelson, and Tiger Woods is testament of short-game wizardry for winning green jackets.

When the PGA Tour comes to Harbor Town the week after the Masters, the tour players play a completely different golf course. The greens at Harbor Town are some of the smallest, and the fairways are some of the tightest of all the PGA Tour. Preparation for playing Harbor Town is completely different than preparation for the Masters. Of course short game matters at any tour event, but the shots played around the greens at Augusta are much different than those at Harbor Town. The tee shots at Augusta allow you to bomb the driver and know you will have large landing areas when the ball lands—unlike Harbor Town, where you might not hit driver on many of the holes. The guys playing week in and week out adjust their games to the conditions and types of course they will play. This is seen throughout the PGA Tour schedule each year.

The West Coast Swing has poa annua greens on the majority of the courses, and the Florida Swing has Bermuda greens on every course. You will often see players at Pebble Beach and Riviera miss short putts on the poa greens that they would rarely miss on the smoother and more consistent Bermuda greens. Some tour players actually change to putters with more loft when playing on the West Coast and go back to their normal putter on the Florida Swing to adapt to each putting surface.

Great players make adjustments according to the conditions they will play during each event.

When you prepare for your club championship or member-guest this year, think about the shots you will need to be successful. If your home course has small greens, you probably don't need to practice long putts. If the superintendent grows the rough longer during these events, you might practice hitting some shots with different lies to see how the ball reacts. If the golf course is played from a longer distance during these events, work on the shots needed from the new distances you would have on your second shots. The key to all of this is being prepared for what you're expecting to see on the golf course *before* you get there.

Dr. Gil Morgan hit those one irons on a hot Oklahoma day, knowing he would need that shot in a few weeks in the cool, damp weather of the British Open. Practice the shots you will need for your major golf events, and you will pull them off when you actually need them.

Pre-Shot Rehearsal

THE FUNCTION OF a rehearsal swing is to create the intended result by doing the opposite of your real swing to reduce your flaw. We've all seen professional golfers making preshot routines before their shot. Why do they do this? They are rehearsing something in their swing they want to have happen during the actual swing. Most rehearsal moves in a golf swing are more extreme than the actual move they want to perform. Billy Horschel takes the club way outside the swing plane during rehearsal, but his actual backswing comes back on a perfect plane. Many tour players make rehearsal swings where they are swinging extreme left. Why would they do this? Most tour players have a tendency to get underneath the swing plane during their downswing, which causes a block or flip of the hands before impact to save the shot. By making extreme swings, the opposite motion of their flaw, they find the correct position.

Next time you watch Miguel Jimenez, Justin Rose, or Graeme McDowell, you will see this extreme downswing move in their rehearsal. The average golfer has the tendency to come over the top and has the opposite problem of the tour player. If you are the player coming over the top, you should make practice swings exactly opposite of that move and rehearse downswings to the far right of your intended line.

Understand your flaws by working with your PGA professional so you can create preshot rehearsals that counterbalance your flaws.

Preparation for Tournament Golf

LAST YEAR I started working with the Sam Houston State Professional Golf Management Program. My job is to work with the students in the program who have not passed their playability test. The playability test is required by the PGA for all their members to pass before they can become a Class A professional. The students know the score they have to shoot before they tee it up.

In all other tournaments, you are trying to beat the players, but in this tournament you are trying to beat a score. It does not matter if you beat everyone you played against; if you don't beat the score, you don't pass. This tournament is a mental test as much as it is a physical test, because the score is always in your mind. Here are some of the ways I prepare these students for this challenge. Hopefully, they can help you with your tournament golf.

The golf swing has to be evaluated and worked on to become as consistent as possible. One thing I am not a believer in is a quick fix. These students are going to get instruction to help their swing for a lifetime. Quick fixes do not hold up under pressure. We look at the swing on video and evaluate the big things in the swing that cause the breakdown. I want my students working on swing changes that will correct the swing, and video is the best way for the student to see this.

The short game is where they all have to work twice as hard as they do on the range. I tell all the students that for every ball you hit on the range, hit two putts and two chips. Phil Mickelson spends countless hours on his short game and hits it all over the golf course but still wins tournaments. You can never spend enough time on your short game if you want to play your best golf.

On-course strategy is essential to see how the student performs in a real situation. I take the players to the first tee and ask them to hit three tee shots. They are told they will be playing the worst ball of the three. They continue this process all the way through the hole, hitting three balls for each shot and playing the worst. This shows me how they handle pressure, as well as the decisions they make on the golf course. Remember, almost all big numbers happen after a poor tee shot, followed by a poor decision.

After these three areas have been evaluated, I make suggestions to the students on where they need to spend more time. The students are given specific drills and training methods to help them pass the player ability test.

It is a blast to work with these kids who have a goal in mind and want to achieve success in the golf business. This is the way I prepare these students for the biggest golf tournament in their careers, and hopefully, it will help you with your next tournament.

Preparing for Sixteen

THIS MORNING WHILE taking my boys to school, my fifteen-year-old son had to listen to every driving scenario he should follow when he gets his driver's license next year. There are numerous pitfalls for a sixteen-year-old when they first get their license, and our insurance rates prove this. When we were entering the highway, my Dad "golf instructor" kicked in, telling him about timing his entrance based on the speed of traffic already on the highway and always making sure his blinker was turned on. We went over this again a few miles down the road for more confirmation when cars were coming off the feeder and onto the highway. We discussed when to slow down and let traffic in or change lanes. My kid told me he had heard all of this before and knew what he was supposed to do when he was able to legally drive. Do all fifteen-year-old boys know more than their dad, or is it just mine? Without hesitation, he was told, "This is all for preparation for when you are old enough to drive. You can never over prepare, and it's my job as your dad to prepare you."

When our young sixteen-year-old children get behind the wheel, they need to have gone through all the possible scenarios they will encounter on the road. They need to know how to parallel park, exit off an interstate, brake properly … and the list goes on. We can have our children trained in every situation, but it doesn't guarantee them not getting into an accident. They can sometimes be in an accident that's not even their fault.

This is all very similar to coaching my students and preparing them for a golf tournament. It's my responsibility to coach the student so they are prepared when they get to the first tee. The driving instructor teaches parallel parking, and the golf coach teaches bunker shots. The golf instructor teaches putting with good speed, and the driving instructor teaches his student to drive the car at the posted speed limit.

The examples could keep going, but the point should be understood by now. The road has hazards everywhere, and the weather can affect how you drive. Sometimes, there are fender benders, but one constant holds true: The better prepared you are, the less likely an accident will happen on the road—and the better you will play on the course.

Prepare for your next tournament the same way you would prepare for your driving exam, and you should have a great round!

Pulled Over

IF YOU DRIVE long enough, you are eventually going to get pulled over by a policeman for speeding. I've unfortunately had this happen on more than one occasion. When you see the lights flashing, your heart usually starts pounding faster, your hands get sweaty, and your body gets tense. You immediately pull over to the side of the road and begin to state your case or your best excuse as to why you were breaking the law. After you've been given a ticket or, hopefully, a warning, I bet you don't step on the gas pedal and drive off fast. You obviously pull out slow and continue to drive the speed limit until you reach your destination.

When I'm on the range, I see people swinging so fast that they have no chance of being consistent. This is just like speeding down the highway in your car, except you are doing it with your golf swing. The more times you swing fast, the more your swing gets out of rhythm. If one of my students gets in this habit, I essentially pull them over. I make them stop what they are doing and have a talk with them about what I see in their swing. They get the golf club back *after* they agree to swing smoother, rather than quick.

Regardless of how good someone swings a golf club, they can't consistently hit good shots when they start swinging too fast. Their hands get sweaty, their body tenses up, and their heart starts to beat faster. Sounds a lot like getting pulled over by a policeman, doesn't it? Before long, the golfer has gone from hitting good shots to going way over the speed limit with their golf swing.

The next time you feel your tempo getting too fast, think about the police officer and the flashing lights. Pull over to the side of the road with your golf swing and take a break. When you start hitting balls again, slow everything down. Drive the speed limit with your golf swing, and you will hit better shots!

Rehearse Your Lines

I'VE ALWAYS BEEN amazed with an actor's ability to remember their lines in a movie. I was recently on a trip with a guy who is best friends with Owen Wilson. We talked about acting and what it takes to be successful in the entertainment industry. He told me how much studying of the script and memorizing of the lines they have to do. It takes a lot of work and discipline for sure to act in a movie.

When golfers set into a shot, they should always have a routine/ rehearsal. Rehearse your routine like you would rehearse lines for a movie. You should have a rehearsal (so to speak) before every shot. If you've rehearsed your lines, this doesn't mean you will get everything perfect on the first take, but your odds will improve. Can you imagine going on a movie set and trying to act *without* rehearsing the script? Many of you do this exact thing on the golf course. You step up to the ball without visualizing the shot or having any idea of what you are trying to do with the shot. I've asked so many people over my twenty-five years of teaching golf, "What's your routine?" I usually receive a vague answer and then never see them perform what they say.

Create a routine that is uniquely yours! If your instructor has given you a new move in your swing, rehearse it until it becomes engrained in your golf swing. Keegan Bradley goes through a list of rehearsal moves before hitting a shot. It drives me nuts to watch him, but he never varies from his rehearsal and has become one of the top players in the game.

The next time you go to the movies, think about how much rehearsing the actors and actresses have done, and apply the same philosophy to your routine before every shot. Visualize and rehearse what you want to happen, and you might win an Academy Award on the links!

Rickie Fowler and Coach McGraw

———— ✺ ————

WHISPERING PINES HOSTS the Big 12 Men's Golf Championship every other year. Sixty of the best golfers in the Big 12 Conference come to compete for four days in April. Each year, we've hosted Oklahoma State, and they always have an all-American roster of players. OSU is known for their golf program and their ability to produce PGA Tour players. Personally, my dream was always to play for the OSU Cowboys, but my game wasn't good enough to get a scholarship. My college golf career went through East Central Oklahoma. The difference playing for ECU vs. OSU was that our team drove in a van to Missouri to play an average golf course while OSU took a private jet from Stillwater to Pebble Beach.

My sister turned out to be the most talented golfer in our family and enjoyed the perks of being an OSU Cowgirl. Even though my golf career wasn't as decorated as hers, I was and still am a super-proud brother of her accomplishments.

The Cowboys arrived on Wednesday for their practice round with their future PGA Tour player Rickie Fowler. Rickie had long hair and looked like Leonardo DiCaprio from the movie *Titanic*. I even started calling him DiCaprio when he was in the clubhouse. Rickie was as genuine as any of the young collegiate players who had come through the gates of Whispering Pines. To date, we've hosted five Big 12 Championships, and I've seen a lot of talented players, but Rickie was special. He had a confidence about him; he knew he was going to win the tournament, and everyone else knew he was going to win the tournament if he played well. He was never arrogant and was very cordial to the staff the entire week.

Coach Mike McGraw is one of the best coaches college golf has ever produced. Our paths have crossed numerous times, from my junior golf days through my sister's time in Stillwater and now with me being the head professional of the course where the Big 12 Championship would be played. Coach McGraw has an infectious smile and is a solid Christian who always treated everyone at Whispering Pines with a grateful attitude and appreciation for us hosting the event.

Rarely do I ever film the college players for my personal library, but every once in a while you have the special player come through who you know will make it to the PGA Tour. Rickie's swing footage is still used for many of my junior golf lessons to this day.

The tournament started on Thursday, with OSU setting the pace as the front-runner. All five of their players had the look of a team destined to win another championship. Individually, Rickie played great all week and looked unstoppable going into the final round.

Coach McGraw had a different coaching style than most coaches. Typically, college golf coaches start on a certain hole and watch all their players come through, and then go to another hole on the course and repeat the process. Coach McGraw always chooses one player to follow for their entire round. I found this interesting and asked what his reasoning might be and what he talked to his players about during the round. He told me that he liked to choose a player he felt might need him that day, and then he would get a consistent feel for their round, rather than jumping back and forth around the course. Rickie looked like he was unstoppable, so I asked Coach McGraw, "What are you going to tell him?"

He said calmly, "Same thing I always ask the player: What's the wind doing? What's the yardage? What type of shot are you going to play?"

This sounded so simple, yet genius as a coaching philosophy. It was almost like the game HORSE in basketball—calling your shot while determining all the factors as if you were playing on an outdoor court.

Rickie Fowler had to call his shot to his coach, along with calculating yardage and wind on every swing. Rickie went on to win the Big 12 Championship at Whispering Pines that day, and the Oklahoma State Cowboys won the team title, as well. When Rickie left the professional shop to head back to Stillwater, I shouted out, "Hey, DiCaprio! See you in two years back at Whispering Pines."

He smiled and gave me the look that his teammates knew as well as I did: He wasn't coming back.

I smiled and said, " See you on the PGA Tour."

He smiled as if to agree without saying a word and boarded the team van.

Rickie Fowler has gone on to a great career as a PGA Tour professional. Everyone on the property knew he would win the Big 12 that week. I've been extremely blessed to work at incredible facilities where so many important people in the golf world come through your club.

I've shared this story with many of my students about Coach McGraw's philosophies with his players. The next time you're on the course, ask yourself what the wind is doing, what's your yardage, and then call your shot. This will keep you accountable every time, just like Coach McGraw kept Rickie Fowler accountable over every shot during the Big 12 Championship.

We all have scars

WHEN I WAS a baby, I underwent a number of surgeries to save my life. By the grace of God and a wonderful surgeon, I'm writing this at the age of forty-five. Every summer when I throw on the bathing suit, I'm reminded of my surgery by the scar on my stomach. It's a reminder to me of how close I came to dying and also a reminder that I've got a purpose to fulfill on this earth.

We all have scars, whether physical or emotional. I went through a painful divorce a few years ago, and it's taken me to this point to feel inspired again and excited about life. We all have a choice on how we react to the bad things that happen to us. We can blame other people, we can think we were dealt a band hand in life, or we can improve and believe our greatest days are ahead of us. Sometimes, bad breaks happen and bad things happen to good people, but that doesn't have to define us.

On the golf course, we also all have scars. When you have missed a lot of putts or hit poor drives, you start to believe in negative outcomes, rather than positive ones. It's easy to believe you are a bad putter or a horrible bunker player if you keep having bad results. So how do you change this mentality and breakdown the golf scar tissue? You have to change your mindset and then work hard to make your putter, sand wedge, driver, or whatever part of your game has scars *better*. If you miss three foot putts and have scars built up over the years about your putting, you need to get your stroke evaluated by a PGA professional. You should talk to your instructor about reading greens and your putting routine, and be honest about the scars you've built up in this area. After your lesson, you have to practice making these changes and start the process of breaking the scar tissue down. The more you properly practice, the more the scars start to go away.

I can look at where I was two years ago and where I am today in my personal life and absolutely know my wounds are healing. Will I always have a physical scar to remind me of my brush with death as a baby? Of course! I'm going to continue to improve in every area of my personal and professional life. We all have a choice on how we handle our scars. I will find someone and marry again. I fully plan on achieving my professional goals. I'll always be thankful for the life I've been given, even with the scar on my stomach.

Recognize your scars today, and make it a point to make a difference in all those areas on the golf course—and life!

The Scorecard and Weight Scale

A NEW GYM recently opened in Huntsville, Texas, last month, and my curiosity got the best of me. My new membership to Anytime Fitness was signed on opening day. All the equipment was brand new, and my motivation to get in great shape was ready and willing. After looking over all the equipment and planning my first workout, I thought it would be good to calculate my weight on their scales. My body isn't too out of shape, but it's important to have a way to measure your progress. The weight scale told me where my workouts (or lack of workouts) stood in relation to my weight on the first day joining the gym.

A scorecard is exactly like a weight scale for your golf game. If you don't keep score, how do you know where your game stands? You can go out and play an entire round without keeping score, but you really don't know what you've shot without a scorecard. All golfers should keep a score every time they play to monitor their progress.

My weight was 184 pounds the first day at the new gym, and I weigh myself after every workout to see if I'm improving. The next time you play golf, keep score to track your progress!

Seat Belt

IT NEVER FAILS. When my teenager gets in my car, he forgets to put on his seat belt. We pull out of the driveway each morning headed to school, and my car starts making this annoying beep. The beep starts at the exact same spot every morning, which is about a half mile into our trip.

Many times, my students will have instructions to add a new preshot routine to combat a flaw they are making. It doesn't matter how many times the new move is discussed; they always forget at some point in the lesson to do it. If we work for an hour on one specific change and then go to the course, it's inevitable they will forget the change made in the lesson at some point on the course. Obviously, with me watching each shot, they have immediate feedback, but how often will they forget once our lesson is over?

This is much like the seat belt beeping when my son is not buckled. If you had a beeping sound to drive you crazy every time you forgot your preshot routine, you would eventually make the change. The merchandise show is held every year in Orlando, and I've yet to see a beeper to alert golfers they are doing something wrong. If someone ever makes one, there will be a few dozen purchased on the spot.

The next time you are working on something your instructor talked about, ask your caddy or one of your playing partners to alert you to the mistake if they notice. I'm sure we will all get a few beeps every round, and hopefully, it saves you from making a bad shot—like a seat belt saves lives.

Self-Fulfilling Prophecy

GOLF PROFESSIONALS LOVE Mondays! This is our one day off to get all our errands taken care of and sometimes play eighteen holes with other golf professionals in the area. At least once a year while working at Colonial, we would get a group of pros and then travel to the Cliffs on Possum Kingdom Lake. This golf course was super cool and was worth the drive to play, especially with a fun gambling group.

We teed it up on a perfect Monday morning and played our way around and over the cliffs. When we reached the back nine, the matches were getting a little intense. We were playing a par-four with a cliff running down the entire right side of the fairway and a few large condos lining the left side. The tee shot was very intimidating, but my game had been really good up to that point. After going through my routine and addressing the ball, I noticed the course marshal pulling up to the tee. It's not unusual for this to happen when club professionals are playing their course. Most of the time, they want to see us hit a shot, thinking we play like Jordan Spieth when we really don't play anything like any of the PGA Tour players. After backing off from the shot and thanking him for the hospitality, the marshal mentioned how many golfers hit the condos on the left side of the fairway. Obviously, he didn't realize he was saying something negative when those words came out of his mouth, but everyone in our group knew my shot had just became tougher.

With my concentration locked in, starting my routine over, my moment of truth was about to happen. My mind was thinking how good this baby fade was going to be with the marshal and my fellow pros watching. There was no doubt the pros in my group thought the house would get hit after the marshal's comment. My backswing was smooth, with a full-shoulder turn, and suddenly, my tempo became quick at the start of my downswing. Coming straight over the top with a shut face at impact, the ball rocketed toward the condo, bouncing off the roof. The marshal put his head down and drove away, knowing his words of choice had not been the best. The pros laughed at my epic failure as another ball was teed up for my third shot with smoke coming out of my ears.

Nobody will ever know if the shot would have been different if the marshal hadn't said those words about the condo, but without question, they were in my head after he mentioned them. The condo was there before the marshal drove up to the tee box and hadn't entered my mind.

The mind is an amazing thing, and our body does what our mind directs it to do.

According to Wikipedia's article on "Self-Fulfilling Prophecy," "A self-fulfilling prophecy is a prediction that directly or indirectly causes itself to become true, by the very terms of the prophecy itself, due to positive feedback between belief and behavior." How many times have you stood over a shot and thought, *Don't hit this ball in the water*? One of two things usually happens when we have this thought: either the ball goes into the water, or the ball is hit the exact opposite direction to avoid the water. Neither shot is conducive for good golf.

When we think of something bad happening on the golf course, it usually happens—or the exact opposite shot happens in the other direction. Our caddies are told to always tell the members where they want them to hit the shot. If a caddie tells you to make sure and stay out of the bunker, what are the chances of you hitting a good shot? You most likely will hit in the bunker or hit the ball the opposite direction of the bunker, because someone put a negative thought in your head.

The next time you play a round of golf, have some positive self-talk. If you are playing by yourself, actually say out loud what type of shot you are going to hit. You can determine your own self-fulfilling prophecy by what you say before each shot.

If you find yourself playing and you see the marshal pull up to the tee, hit your shot before he starts telling you where all the bad golfers hit theirs!

Shadow great players

———— ❧ ————

ONE OF MY standout students over the past decade has been Will Griffin. Will had a determination and work ethic to be great. His desire to play golf at the highest level was evident the first day we met. Through the years, it was fun watching him grow physically and mentally in his golf game. His dream after high school was always to play for the University of Texas. That dream came true when he signed his letter of intent to play for the Longhorns in his senior year of high school.

The next session we had after his signing, he was decked out in burnt-orange. He had reached one of his dreams and had all the cool gear to prove he had arrived as a Longhorn. Will was an ultra-competitive person, which you have to be to reach that level of the game. He was a goal setter and spent his time on the range honing his skills. Some of the coolest moments as a teacher come late in the afternoon when the sun is working its way down, and it's just you and your student on the back of range. Will hit some of the purest shots on many of those late evenings. I'm rarely in awe of anyone's ball striking, but there were times where it was a thing of beauty to watch.

Will's freshman year at Texas also had the signing of a kid from Dallas named Jordan Spieth. Nobody knew how good Jordan was going to be, and neither did I at the time, but we all knew he was something special. Jordan had played in the Spirit International at Whispering Pines when he was still in high school. His maturity as he spoke to reporters about playing for his country was the same as it is today when he gives a speech after a tour event or major championship.

When I was playing golf in college, we always sized up the incoming freshmen. When Jordan arrived at The University of Texas, there was no question he was going to be an impact player immediately. Will and I discussed Jordan during numerous sessions. Cameron McCormick and I have a mutual friendship as teachers in Texas. I've always admired Cameron; the success he's had did not come by chance. He has produced so many great players and should definitely go down as one of the best teachers of this decade.

One of the challenges I gave to Will when Jordan arrived was to pay attention to everything he did on and off the golf course. There's an old saying that if you want to be a great putter, hang out with great putters. This is exactly what I was telling Will to do. Players should never be in awe of each other, but they can learn a lot by watching and asking questions. One of the very unique things about the game of golf is that most of the time, players are willing to help other players. You see this on the PGA Tour all the time—and rarely (if ever) see it in any other sport. When you have the opportunity to be around someone who has separated themselves in whatever field or sport they are in, you should pay attention. Can you imagine being a guitarist and having the opportunity to hang out with Eddie Van Halen for a couple years? This was an opportunity for Will to spend time every day with a golfer who was destined to be on the PGA Tour.

My instructions to Will were to go to the short-game area with Jordan, play practice rounds with Jordan, ask him how he hits certain shots, and shadow him in every way on and off the course. This wasn't to make Will feel inferior but to show him what an opportunity he had in front of him. Jordan realistically was only going to be in school for a few years. I told Will this would be the equivalent of a young Tiger Woods becoming his teammate. (Texas went on to win a national championship, and Jordan went on to the PGA Tour two years later.)

I'm sure every golfer on that University of Texas golf team for those two years learned something by watching Jordan Spieth. When you play with great players, you don't have to be in awe, but you should pay attention to what they do better than others on the course. The next time you're on the range and the club champion is hitting balls, watch what he does. Try to schedule a friendly game with some of the best players at your club and pay attention to how they play the game. When you hang out with good players, it can rub off on your own game. If you get a chance to play with the Jordan Spieth of your club, make sure and ask him if you can tee it up with him sometime. I guarantee you will learn something by playing with better players.

Slow Greens and Fast Greens

GARY PLAYER PLAYED in a tournament where the greens were very slow. When he finished his round, everyone in the locker room was complaining about how slow the greens were. Gary said, "I love slow greens." A few weeks later, Gary player played in a tournament where the greens were extra fast. Everyone in the locker room was complaining about how fast the greens were. Gary Player said, "I love putting on fast greens." One of the players in the locker room who had heard his comments at the other tournament (where he'd said he loved slow greens) called him out on his statement. The player said to Gary, "You said a few weeks ago you love slow greens, and now you say to everybody in the locker room you love fast greens."

Gary Player said, "I love whatever green speed I'm putting on."

The moral to the story is to love whatever the course conditions give you, because everyone is playing the same conditions. The people who complain are the easiest to beat. Accept the speed of the greens, and love whatever the putting surface happens to be in every tournament.

What's Most Important in Putting: Line or Speed?

―――― ∞ ――――

IF YOU HAVE a thirty-foot putt and strike the ball on the perfect line, but your speed left the ball ten feet short, you would have a ten-foot putt left.

If you have a thirty-foot putt and strike the ball three feet off line with perfect speed, you would have a three-foot putt left.

Answer: Speed is the most important part of putting.

Speed and Tempo

THE DIFFERENCE IN speed and tempo is very similar to a drummer keeping a drumbeat. The drummer for a hard-rock band like Metallica plays differently than the drummer for George Strait. They both keep a consistent rhythm and tempo during each song, but their speed will differ. All golfers have a rhythm to their swing. Some of us have a Metallica type of rhythm, and some of us have a George Strait type of rhythm. The key to both is having a *consistent* tempo!

Don't Spill the Sand

RECENTLY WHILE SANDING a divot, I had a thought come to mind about how to start the backswing. I noticed when I held the sand bottle and made a proper move on my takeaway, I didn't spill any sand. When I made a poor takeaway, sand fell out of the bottle.

The key to a good backswing is getting the club started on the correct path in the beginning. If you take the club too far to the inside, you will have trouble setting the club in the proper position at the top of the swing. Conversely, if you start the club on the proper path in the beginning, it's much easier to set the club in a good position at the top of backswing.

Look at the following pictures and see the difference on the good position where the sand stays in the bottle versus the hand position when the sand falls out. Next time you sand a divot, try this simple drill to feel the correct position of the takeaway!

Staying Positive Despite
the Circumstances

EVERY YEAR AT the end of our spring season, we have a Ryder Cup match within our club. We split the state in half and determine a south and north team. I try to create as much animosity as possible in a professional way between the teams. I'm the captain of the north and our general manager is the captain of the south. We even split the cottages from one side of the road to the other to create more of a rivalry. For one weekend at Whispering Pines, the membership is divided, and it's usually touted to be the most fun event of the season.

When the tournament is over, the winner doesn't get a trophy or plaque. They get a champagne flute filled with sparkling champagne, and the losing team has to watch the winning team have a celebratory toast.

One of my members and good buddies, Billy Quinn, teed it up together in the best ball format. Billy and I have a love for 80s hair bands. We are the same age; we both want Sammy Hagar back in Van Halen and always enjoy each other's company when we play golf. The round started off with us getting the tunes ready and game faces on to beat the south team we were playing against. We had a great match going back and forth throughout the first eight holes, but found ourselves down in the match when we arrived at the 9th hole. Billy hit his tee ball, and it was less than stellar for his standards. Driving has never been my greatest strength, and I proved it to my teammate and the other team as I snap-hooked my drive into the heavy rough, as well.

When Billy got in the cart, he was upset because we had both hit poor tee shots and our opponents were in prime position. Even worse, we were going to lose the point for the front nine if we didn't somehow pull off a miracle.

Billy was vocalizing to me his frustration and basically was conceding the match in his mind. I looked at Billy and said, "Do you have any idea how much this is going to demoralize them when we find a way to win this hole?"

Billy looked at me with a big smile and said, "You're right. Let's go win this hole!"

Billy hit a nice shot to get back into play and was left with eighty yards to a back-left pin. The other team looked like they had us beat when Billy stuck a sand wedge to six feet. With a big right-to-left sliding putt, we still had no guarantee of winning even after the great shot. Billy stood over the putt and took a few practice strokes while looking at the hole. He addressed the putt and made one of the silkiest strokes I've ever seen. The ball rolled off the putter blade and dropped in the bottom of the cup! Our opponents looked at us in utter disgust while trying to crack a smile as they said, "Good putt."

The momentum had shifted, and we both played great golf from that point forward, winning all of the remaining points.

There are always moments in a round of golf or sporting event where the momentum shifts. It can be a good break or a change in attitude that makes all the difference and creates a momentum change. On that day, a simple kick in the butt from the pro telling my member we would not lose this match regardless of our circumstances made the difference. We were both in the woods, our opponents were both in great position, and it looked like we had no chance to win. The match changed when we made the decision to stay positive and expect to win, rather than give up and lose. The greatest discovery in modern psychology is that people become what they think. On that day, we chose to think like winners and wouldn't accept anything less. The next time you are in the woods or have a difficult shot, remember this story. When you stand over that difficult shot, think to yourself about how cool it's going to be when you make birdie and your opponents have already written you off!

The Golf-Swing Gap Theory

RECENTLY, I CAME across a new idea to determine how consistent or inconsistent a golfer plays based on the gap they create between backswing and downswing. I call this the "swing gap." The wider the swing gap, the more timing and tempo is required. The tighter the swing gap, the less timing is required for consistent ball striking. If you look at Fred Couples's swing, you will quickly notice the amount of swing gap he creates between his backswing and downswing. Freddie has beautiful tempo and has hit millions of golf balls, perfecting his swing, but he does have unique positions. From the pictures of his swing, you will notice the yellow line shows the path of his backswing, and the red line shows the path of his downswing. He has one of the widest swing gaps I've seen from a professional golfer, but his tempo is so smooth he makes the game look easy!

Davis Love has an almost no gap between his backswing and downswing. When you have your swing gap as tight as Davis's, your ball striking is usually very consistent and solid. Notice the yellow line for his backswing and how close the red line matches on his downswing. Davis can move through the ball very fast and not have to rely on timing as much to play well.

Tiger actually has two different swing gaps. Years ago, I wrote an article that has become my teaching theory: "Target Impact & Rounded Impact." Tiger impacts differently with a driver than with his irons. Tiger has a target impact position with his driver and a rounded impact position with his irons. You will notice the gap is much wider with his driver than it is with his irons.

The swing gap doesn't always put you in one certain impact position, but the wider swing gap players tend to be target impact. The tighter swing gap players tend to fall into the rounded impact category.

If your instructor uses video, ask him to draw your lines on backswing and downswing. See how much swing gap you have and decide which direction you want to take your impact position. If you need a refresher on target impact and rounded impact, go to www.whisperingpinesgolfclub.com and look at my article, which was published in *Houston Links Magazine* a few years ago.

Tell Me Something Good!

A FEW MONTHS ago, a lady came to take her first lesson from me. The standard first lessons always involve questions to get to know the new student before critiquing the swing. As my list of questions started, it didn't take long to realize she had taken numerous golf lessons in her life. She told me all the problems she had with her swing and what all the instructors before me had said about her swing. She also mentioned she had been up since 3:00 a.m. thinking about her driver swing and her upcoming lesson.

Numerous red flags started to pop up in my analysis before the actual instruction was to start. This lady had been a high jumper, swimmer, and now a golfer. She was ultra-competitive and had obsessive-compulsive tendencies, as well.

Once we started hitting shots, she critiqued every ball flight and mentioned all the things she had done wrong with each swing. Adjustments were made, and she started hitting better shots, and after twenty minutes, her ball flight had become noticeably different. Even though all the shots she hit were much better than her shots earlier in the lesson, she could still find something wrong.

When a student gets into these negative patterns, I make them verbally say a positive comment after each shot. She looked at me, puzzled, but agreed to give me a positive affirmation on the next shot. The next shot was a topped ball that rolled about 120 yards down the range, but she verbally expressed that the shot rolled a long way. The next shot was a high push to the right of her target, and she mentioned how solid the ball was hit.

After a few more swings with positive affirmations after each shot, her shot patterns started getting better. Before long, in her verbal analysis of each shot, it was easy to find something good because the shots were good.

Many times we start getting down on ourselves because of this game. Yes … it's a game! I doubt any of you reading this story base your salary on how you hit a golf ball. Golf is already going to beat you up, so why beat yourself up by verbally abusing yourself after every shot that's not up to your standards? In a round of golf, if you hit three to five great shots, you're ahead of the field. Golf is a game of misses, and where you miss determines what you shoot.

Next time you hit a poor shot, find something good about that shot and verbalize it. The more you do this, the more you will start to see the good in other things, as well. The worst day of golf is still better than a day in the office. Enjoy the game more during your next round and find something positive to say about every shot!

Tension

TENSION IS SOMETHING we've all experienced at some point on the golf course. When we have tension, we tend to breathe faster, grip the club tighter, and our tempo becomes quicker than normal. What causes tension? The main cause is putting too much emphasis on a shot. Years ago, I would take a Pro-Am team to the Byron Nelson 11th Straight Tournament. Knowing my name would be announced on the first tee—with lots of people watching—created enormous amounts of tension hours before the shot would actually be struck. Making the shot bigger than it actually was wasn't going to help me hit a great drive. Fortunately, the tee shot was ripped down the middle with some of the techniques discussed in the following story.

A few weeks ago one of my members, who had been playing great golf for weeks, was hitting the ball erratically on the range before his round. It was obvious he was swinging faster than normal, and you could see the amount of tension he was carrying in his shoulders and chest. I walked over and started giving him some tips and realized immediately when grabbing his club how tight he was holding the grip. We worked on numerous issues without much success when I asked him who he was playing with; he mentioned the names, with everyone carrying a low handicap. The tension was coming from what he thought about his game compared to the rest of the group—my member didn't have a low handicap and was concerned about embarrassing himself on the golf course.

My instruction immediately went to getting rid of the tension. I told him those guys didn't care how he played but *did* care about the comradery and enjoyment they would have playing Whispering Pines with him. It's easy to think everyone in your foursome is critiquing your game when the reality is they are only concerned about their own game. My advice was light grip pressure and to make a 70 percent swing with every club. He set up the ball, exhaled, and made the smoothest swing he had made all morning. The ball rocketed off the face of the club and sailed to the target, landing next to the flag. He turned and looked at me in amazement, realizing at that moment he could play well if he got rid of the tension. He hit shot after shot with his new tension-free swing and shook my hand as we walked off the range together. As he approached his cart, I stopped him and told him, "Nobody cares how you hit the ball, so go have fun."

After the round, he sought me out to tell me how well he had played and thanked me for the tune-up.

We all want to play good every time we tee it up. We might have tension because of the group we are playing in or a famous golf course we are playing at—or we might be playing the best round of our lives and don't want to screw it up. Whatever the reason, tension can creep in and can destroy a round. Remember, when you feel tension in your swing, take a deep breath, grip the club lightly, and make a 70 percent swing. If you do this, you will play a better round guaranteed!

The Ten-Thousand-Hour Rule

※

RECENTLY, I WAS looking through my book *He Who Looks Up Shall See a Bad Shot* and came across a story I had written titled "My Advice to the Fallen Tour Player." This story was written about six years ago, and it discussed the possibility of Tiger Woods losing his game. As I skimmed through the story, it was almost prophetic. Tiger Woods has undoubtedly lost his golf game, and the mental edge he once had is now gone. How did this happen? Why does this happen to so many players on the PGA Tour? Well, you're going to have to read the book to find out. *This* story is about the ten-thousand-hour rule, but it does apply to Tiger Woods trying to regain his golf game.

There are two books that go into great detail about the ten-thousand-hour rule: *Outliers: The Story of Success* and *Talent Is Overrated*. These books have completely changed the way I think about coaching and teaching students. For those of you who are not familiar with the ten-thousand-hour rule, it's the belief that a skill has to be performed for at least ten thousand hours to become mastered. A common theme among athletes, musicians, and many other professions is ten thousand hours of deliberate practice. Notice I said *deliberate* practice. This also means being coached and watched on a consistent basis through the ten thousand hours in the process. You see this with gymnasts, musicians, and golfers. Even Bill Gates spent ten thousand hours writing code and learning about computers.

If you practiced twenty hours a week for roughly ten years, you could hit the ten-thousand-hour rule. This isn't going out and hitting golf balls to warm up and then playing eighteen holes. This is working twenty hours a week on specific things in your golf swing under the eye of a good coach. I thought about this in my own profession and realized I probably reached the ten-thousand-hour rule in teaching golf at about the age of thirty-four.

When someone has completed ten thousand hours, they see things faster and can make a judgment call or change in a golf swing much faster than someone who hasn't reached the magical number. For instance, if I am giving a golf lesson, and a PGA professional, who just graduated through a professional golf management college, is giving a golf lesson to the same student, we both would most likely see the same flaw in the student's swing. The person who's completed ten thousand hours of teaching sees the correction and the solution differently from the younger instructor. The student is coming over the top and pulling all his shots left. The younger instructor would have the solution to change the downswing to correct the swing path. The more experienced teacher would notice that the golfer was not shifting his weight properly and not making a full shoulder turn, which causes him to lean toward the target on his downswing and change the angle and steepness of his impact. Each instructor would come to the same conclusion on the flaw, but the given instruction would be different.

The more experience, the better you become at your profession. Would you want to have major surgery from a doctor who just graduated medical school, or have a surgeon who has performed thousands of surgeries?

Now, let's talk about Tiger Woods. It is thought that Tiger Woods most likely reached the ten-thousand-hour rule around the age of nineteen. It is remarkable to put in that many hours of practice and reach his skill level by that age—but remember that his father was Earl Woods. Earl had Tiger hitting golf balls when he was barely out of his highchair. If you look at Tiger's coaching, he had Butch Harmon through his teenage years. Tiger Woods is a perfect example of deliberate practice and great coaching. He is the model for the ten-thousand-hour rule!

Lately, we watch Tiger Woods have chipping problems, driver problems, and scoring problems. It's actually very sad to watch one of the greatest golfers of all time look like a heavyweight fighter past his prime. Tiger talks about motor patterns and being stuck between swings. Tiger has already put in ten thousand hours with the Butch Harmon swing. It's quite possible he put in another ten thousand hours of practice under Hank Haney. With his body breaking down and having two different instructors in the past two years, I do not believe it's possible for him to get another ten thousand hours of practice to make the changes he needs to become great again.

My advice to Tiger: Go back to your Butch Harmon or your Hank Haney swing and stick with it until you retire from the game. You don't have enough years or time to spend practicing something new.

I truly hope Tiger regains his form and competes at a high level again. Whether you like Tiger or dislike Tiger, he still moves the needle in the game of golf!

The Clean House

My mother always kept a clean house, and this has stuck with me throughout my life. We had to make our beds every morning before school and dust the furniture once a week. I've tried to continue these habits with my own children. I'm not a clean freak, where you pull out the microscope to look for dirt, but I do like things to be in order.

One thing I've noticed about keeping my house clean is that the more I stay on top of the cleaning, the less there is to clean. If you wait for the laundry to pile up, then you will have a lot of laundry to do at one time. If you leave dishes or neglect to sweep the floors, it doesn't take long for the house to look cluttered and dirty. I try to do a little bit every day, and the house always seems to be in good shape. Obviously, if I have guests coming over, the house will be cleaner than normal, but my home should always be presentable if a guest stops by unannounced.

Practice sessions for your golf swing could be compared to cleaning your home. Many people let their swing get messy. They end up having a lot to clean up when they decide their swing is a mess. Some people pay a housekeeper, due to time restraints and busy work schedules. This is much like hiring a golf instructor to work with you. If you have a professional helping you clean up your swing, it's much easier than trying to do it on your own. The longer you let your house go without a good cleaning, the more work it's going to take to make it look good. The same is true with letting your golf swing go for months without getting a look from your golf professional. The same is true of daily practice on all areas of your game.

Don't limit your work to just one area of your game. When you do this, it's like keeping the kitchen clean and neglecting the bathroom. When you practice, you should work on every part of your game throughout the week. Hit balls on the range and chip one day. The next day, work on your putting and bunker game. When you have an upcoming tournament, you want a deep cleaning. Get with your instructor, carve out a couple hours a day, and spend enough time preparing for your event. If you were going to host a big party at your home, you wouldn't start preparing the night before, and you shouldn't start preparing for a tournament the day before.

When your house is clean, it makes you feel good, and when your golf game is clean, you feel good! Clean up your swing on a daily basis, and it will never become a mess! I'm going to go clean my house as soon as I finish this article!

The Day My Dad Set Me Straight

As a youthful young lad cursed with a bad temper and thinking very highly of my golf skills, my dad set me straight on a hot July day in Oklahoma. The 9th hole at Tishomingo Golf Course was the first time my father taught me a lesson. This wasn't the instructional golf tip on getting the club in the correct positions, either! In front of our foursome, it was my opinion that I needed to act like an idiot and have a temper tantrum after a poor shot. For some reason, this seemed like a good thing to do, since my golf game was so refined—or so I thought! This was embarrassing for my dad, and I was too stupid at the time to realize it was an embarrassment for me. My dad took my clubs after we walked off the 9th green and said this would be the last round of golf I would play for a week.

Golf was my life and passion, and the week of suspension seemed like a year. This was such a great lesson at a young age. You see this all the time with parents and their children, but most the time, the parents do not reprimand the child. If my dad wouldn't have done this to me, I promise this behavior would have happened again.

The second time my dad set me straight was my junior year of high school. The band Stryper was playing at the Lloyd Noble Center in Norman, and it happened to be the same day as a golf tournament. The reasonable thing to do in my opinion was to play the tournament and go to the concert. The tournament would end around 5:00 in the afternoon, and the concert started at 7:00. This was perfect because my friends were going to pick me up from the course and drive to the concert. My round of golf was absolutely horrible, mainly because I was thinking about seeing the concert. My heart wasn't in the tournament, and it was pathetic the way I played—and my score was even more embarrassing. The worst part was how well my previous tournament had gone. The previous week, I had shot the lowest back nine in field, and many people, along with my coach, thought I might win the next event.

I've always wanted to be a rock star and was playing in a band at the time. Concerts have always been something I've enjoyed, and to this day, I try and go to as many as possible. The problem back then was that the opportunity to get a college scholarship to play golf was very real. Our band wasn't going on tour with the Rolling Stones anytime soon, and my practice habits were not as good when the rock band was practicing on Sunday. Don't get me wrong: Playing in a band is a rush and one of the most enjoyable things I've ever done. But it wasn't making me a better golfer!

The next morning, my dad woke me up very early and asked what I had shot. He already knew the answer but wanted me to explain this to him at 6:30 a.m. He said in a very stern and serious tone, "Do you want to be a rock star or get a golf scholarship?" He was correct, because it was impossible to play in a band and devote enough time to my golf game. I gave up the rock band that week and focused on golf, and the following year, I received a golf scholarship to East Central University. Guitars and music are still a passion of mine, but golf became a career.

Thanks, Dad, for the kick in the butt and for helping me understand the bigger picture! Love you!

The Goal

I'M ALWAYS TRYING to get creative with my lessons, so this week I told one of my young junior golfers to meet me at the soccer field. I took a shag bag and asked him to hit shots from seventy yards into the goal. I asked him to visualize the ball bouncing in for a score. I then moved him ten yards away to work on trajectory. He had to hit six irons through the goal and couldn't go above the beam. The purpose of this drill was to keep the ball low for those times when you're in the woods and have to punch out—and those windy days when you need to flight your ball lower than normal.

When we finished the lesson, I told him he would understand and remember this lesson for years! Next time you pass by a soccer field or watch the World Cup, think of this lesson.

Short Game

Chipping: Hands forward

>   Ball played off of right big toe
>   Majority of weight on left side
>   Club never gets ahead of hands
>   Maximum ground time, minimum air time

Pitching: Hands forward

>   Ball played center of stance
>   Accelerate through shot
>   Turn through shot

Bunkers: Middle of stance

>   Weight on left side
>   Pick club up with right hand
>   Look at sand, not ball
>   Accelerate through shot
>   Face of club points toward target
>   Bunker shots are all right hand

Flop Shots: Choke down

>   Middle of stance
>   Weight on left side
>   Accelerate through impact
>   Clubface faces target

Quotes to Remember

"Great shots are like great friends: Everybody has friends, but great friends are hard to come by. If you have more than three, you're lucky."

"He who looks up shall see a bad shot."

"Practice with a purpose. How many times have you told someone, 'I hit it great on the range,' but can't take it to the golf course?"

"When you practice, always aim at a target. Have you ever gone to shoot baskets and aimed at the backboard?"

"When flexing your knees, make sure you can still see your feet. If you can't see your feet, you have flexed too much."

"We are all stuck with our own swing flaws. The key is manage those flaws."

"It is physically impossible to hit a golf ball thin if you take a divot."

The Haircut

When Whispering Pines reopens, I always want my staff to get a haircut before our members walk through the door. As I write this, it's evident I've waited too long myself and need to get my hair trimmed. All of you reading this usually will go to your barber or stylist and get a haircut before a big meeting or important date on your calendar. If you are bald, just humor me and finish the story.

The longer we wait, the more gel we have to put in our hair to make it look presentable. Before long, you might be putting more grease in your hair than in your car!

I knew a guy when I worked at Colonial who got his hair cut every two weeks. Colonial has a barber shop next to the golf shop, so we would regularly see our members getting their hair cut. Some people would get their hair cut and look totally different because they had waited so long, but the member who went every two weeks always looked the same. It didn't matter what time of year or what the weather was doing, this member sat down in the barber's chair every two weeks and got his hair cut.

This got me thinking about golfers who take lessons only when they need help and the ones who meet me on the lesson tee every time they come to Whispering Pines. Many golfers let their games grow hairy and have to use gel (so to speak) on their swings to get around the course.

When people put off taking the lesson they know they need, their games become a mess. When the golfer finally sits down in the PGA professional's barber chair—the teaching tee—and takes a lesson, they leave looking different. Then there's the guy who shows up every two weeks, like the Colonial member, and works with his instructor. When you see him on the range or playing on the course, he never really looks any different. His tempo and fundamentals have very little difference from week to week. If you have the ability to see your instructor on a regular basis, your swing will stay consistent, and you will have more fun on the course. People who continually try to educate themselves and get better usually come out on top in all fields. Golfers who take lessons on a regular basis are getting education on how to hit the ball better and create better and more consistent fundamentals. Jordan Spieth has his instructor at every major, and I'm sure sees him when he is back in Dallas for regular maintenance.

The best players all go to their swing coach on a regular basis.

The next time you sit down in your barber's chair, pick up the phone and schedule that lesson with your pro—and don't wait till your game needs extra hair gel to keep it in place!

The Knockout Punch

I'VE GOT TO admit I love watching the new series *Ultimate Fighter*. I seldom watch television and rarely get hooked on a show, but this one has me watching every week. The team captains pick a fighter each week to go up against the other team's fighter. The fights are very intense, and knockouts are plentiful. I'm not a violent person and have never personally been in a fight, but I do want to beat up my bag every once in a while on the golf course.

There are a few analogies I made from watching this show that go hand in hand with golf. First, there is the submission hold, where the fighters tap out when their opponent gets them in a position where the pain is too much. On the golf course, I can think of numerous times where players should have submitted, rather than kept fighting. How many times have you been in the trees and had an easy pitchout back to the fairway, but decided to keep fighting while hitting numerous trees? If you know you are in a submission situation and you can't see any way out, pitch it out of the trees or whatever type of trouble you are in.

The second analogy is the knockout punch. Most of the fighters try and land a big shot once they feel like they are losing. Usually, this results in a mistake, and the fighter usually gets in more trouble by trying to make the big shot rather than sticking to the game plan. Golfers tend to do this when they feel they need to make up ground, and they take chances they shouldn't try and take. How many times have you made a couple of bogeys in a row or made a big number on a hole and then tried too hard to birdie the next hole? When golfers try to do this, they normally get knocked out on the scorecard. Knockouts should be calculated and executed at the correct time in the round. You don't have to score a knockout to win a tournament or to have a good round. When you try too hard to make something happen, it almost always doesn't work out.

All of you golfers who watch *Ultimate Fighter* pay attention to what the winners do when they enter the cage and see how it correlates to watching the PGA Tour. The best golfers in the world don't make eagles on every par-five, but take calculated risks when the time is right. The best golfers in the world also know when a submission hold has been placed on them, and tap out. I'm not promoting fighting, but I am promoting better golf scores!

The Match

EVERY YEAR, COLONIAL would receive an invitation to the Byron Nelson 11th Straight Pro-Am at the Four Seasons at Las Colinas. This was always a fun couple of days with my members, staying at a wonderful resort and playing in the tournament. The best part of the event was spending time with Mr. Byron Nelson. He would attend the functions and even come out to the course to watch. Talk about getting nervous when Mr. Nelson showed up to see you hit a shot!

The most memorable moment of the event was always the time we spent at his ranch. He invited every team out to his ranch and even allowed us to walk through his home to see all his trophies. Mr. Nelson was an absolute gentleman and was happy to answer questions and talk to all of us. He told us numerous stories about Ben Hogan and their relationship. He talked about the major championships and the scores he had shot to win.

The question that I most wanted to ask was the mythical story I had heard for years about the match at Cypress Point. I gathered my team around and asked Mr. Nelson if he would tell us about the day he and Hogan played Harvey Ward and Ken Venturi. He was sitting on a bench and began telling the story like it happened yesterday. He talked about the weather and the beauty of Cypress Point. Mr. Nelson went through the entire round, with all of us hanging on every word. The foursome that day had twenty-six birdies and one eagle at Cypress Point.

In my teaching facility, there is a picture of a young twenty-nine-year-old golf professional and Mr. Nelson taken right before he told us the story of the match. Over a decade later, a book was written, titled *The Match*. When people ask if I've read the book chronicling the greatest four-ball ever played, I just smile and say, "I've heard it's a great book."

The Orange and the Apple

HOW MANY TIMES have you had someone tell you to block out a bad thought in your head? You are on the tee box, and there is out of bounds down the right side. You say to yourself, *I'm going to block that out of bounds out of my head.* What usually happens is the golf shot goes ten miles left of the trouble—or goes right in the trouble.

I heard the saying "Just block it out" so many times over my career, and I haven't blocked anything except my driver.

The truth is you can't block out thoughts, but you can replace them with something else. I do this with my students all the time, and it absolutely works.

I want you to close your eyes right now and think of an orange. This orange was just picked off a tree in Florida. You can smell the orange right now. Your mouth is watering just thinking about this juicy orange.

Now open your eyes!

Now close your eyes again, and I want you to think of a big, juicy apple. This apple was just picked off a tree in Washington. The texture of this apple is perfect, and the color is vivid red. Can you see the apple?

Where did the orange go?

The orange was simply replaced by the apple. You didn't block it out; you simply thought of something else. When you are on the 18th tee at Pebble Beach, you can't block the ocean out or make it go away. The ocean waves are crashing against the rock wall, and it's physically in front of you. The fairway is also physically in front of you. The ocean is the orange, and the fairway is the apple. You can choose which one you are going to focus on and then play the shot. The incredible thing about our minds is we can choose what we want to think about, and our bodies will react to our thoughts.

The next time you see trouble off the tee, focus on the orange-and-apple drill. Replace all the bad thoughts with positive ones and get an apple at the turn!

The Par-Five

PAR-FIVES ARE THE longest holes on the golf courses we play. In theory, and most of the time by handicap, they play tougher than the majority of the other holes on the course. One thing I've noticed is that you don't have to hit three great shots to reach the green. When you hit a big tee shot, you're usually left with the decision to lay up or go for the green. When you hit a poor tee shot, your decision is made for you. Poor tee shots on par-fives don't allow you to go for the green; they force you into a layup shot. When you hit an average or poor tee shot on the longest holes on the course, I've found that most of my students make par more often than when they hit a big tee shot and go for the green. I'm not saying hitting a great tee shot is a bad thing, but the decision, accompanied by the risk, can bring in bigger numbers on the scorecard. Remember, the next time your tee shot on a par-five isn't great, it could actually be an advantage!

The Perfect Golf Swing

DOES THE PERFECT golf swing exist? My answer is there is no such thing as a perfect golf swing, but everyone has a perfect golf swing in them. Would anyone say that Jordan Spieth has a perfect golf swing? Many golf instructors would say technically no, but he has a green jacket in his closet. How about Jim Furyk? David Feherty once said his swing looked like an octopus falling out of a tree. Jim Furyk has a US Open trophy in his house. The question is, what is the perfect golf swing? The answer is, your perfect golf swing is the swing you can repeat. Lee Trevino hit thousands of golf balls every day with an open stance and pronounced loop. Trevino is regarded as one of the greatest ball strikers of all time. Byron Nelson once said to find a swing you can repeat and spend the rest of your life working on it.

Parents bring their children to golf instructors every day, wanting little Johnny to become the next Jordan Spieth or Rory McIlory. Cameron McCormick, Jordan's instructor, has done a marvelous job with his star student. Many teachers would have made changes, and the results most likely wouldn't have produced the spectacular player Jordan has become. I'm not saying every kid needs to swing like Bubba Watson. I *am* saying the best instructors know what to say and what not to say.

We host the Big 12 Championship and the Spirit International at Whispering Pines every two years. I've seen the best players in the world come through our gates over the past ten years. The player with the technically perfect golf swing rarely won these events. When Jordan played the Spirit International, we had seventy-three national champions on our driving range. Every morning, I watched the players warm up for their rounds, and they all struck the ball very well. While watching Jordan, I very much admired him as a player and knew his

145

accomplishments, but he didn't stand out over any of the others. When you saw Jordan on the *course*, it was a completely different story. He had a passion to win like very few I've seen. On the course, he did stand out more than any player, and the United States went on to win the Spirit International that year.

Not everyone's body can do what Dustin Johnson can, so why should you try to swing like him? All golfers have DNA in their swing, and the swing will have a certain look. The next time you take a lesson, talk to your instructor about the swing that will hold up under pressure and repeat for a lifetime. If you find that swing, you are going to have a lot of fun on the golf course this year!

The Pete Effect

Do you have that certain person who has your number when you are paired together? The golfer whom you just can't seem to beat? It can be a personality difference, pace of play, anger issues, or maybe just the fact that you don't like the person. Tiger and Phil never cared for each other, and it was evident during the Ryder Cup when Hal Sutton paired them together. It can also be the case when the player has continually beaten you every time you have played against them. Look at the players who've been paired with Tiger when he was in his prime—and completely fallen apart shooting embarrassing scores.

My Achilles heel has always been Pete Matthews from the Wade Hampton Golf Club. Pete is a wonderful professional, and I truly have the utmost respect for him. We get along great and have played numerous rounds together over the past seven years during the Challenge Cup. Whispering Pines plays the Wade Hampton Club every year in July at their place, and they come to Texas to play us in November at the Pines. The weather is always spectacular in the mountains of North Carolina in the summer, and November in Texas is perfect, as well. It's always a fun weekend of great food, camaraderie, and golf at the Challenge Cup.

Pete has always been an exceptional player and prides himself on shooting low scores. He has played in tour events and won numerous section events.

When we play our match with Wade Hampton, we always play at least two of the three matches together. The last day of the Challenge Cup, Pete and I always play head to head in the singles match. The most points won by the Whispering Pines pro in all the years of playing him has been half a point—out of a possible three points. It doesn't matter how much practice or how well my game has been, our results have been the same.

Golf is a funny game and can humble you at any time, as we all know. In high school, my game allowed me to earn all-state honors in my junior and senior years. It was so much fun for me to play tournaments and challenge myself back in the day. As Father Time has caught up with me, my game has seen some dry spells. PGA professionals run events, teach the game, merchandise, and run the golf operations at their respective clubs. There is a huge difference between a golf professional and professional golfer! My living isn't based on how low my score was on Saturday with the members or what score was posted in the Pro-Pro in our section event. Our job as PGA professionals is to make our members' experiences special every time they come to the club. This doesn't keep me from wanting to be competitive and playing the game at the high level it once produced, but it does become more difficult when the responsibilities of our job outweigh working on our game.

The format for the first day is always "best ball" matches in the morning and "alternate shot" in the afternoon. The weather was magical as we all warmed up on the range Saturday morning. My shots were crisp, and the swing felt fluid as the range balls sailed toward the target.

Before leaving the range, it's my standard routine to hit the club and the type of shot required for my first tee shot of the day. My hybrid, with a slight draw, was perfect just before we made our way to the first hole to begin the match. We all shook hands on the first tee and wished each other luck. Pete striped one down the middle, as usual, and then it was my turn. The routine was exactly like my shots on the range; my breathing technique, visualization, and everything that I've taught all my students over the years was executed perfectly. Addressing the ball, there were no nerves or anxiety, only excitement about the round. My club moved back slowly, but my transition into my downswing was much quicker than it had been just five minutes earlier. The club struck the ball off the toe of the club, and in horror, I watched it snap hook into the hazard. This shot could not have been anything further from my practice session. I stood in disbelief and embarrassment, knowing my round had started this way.

The rest of the round was pathetic, with my team losing three points that morning. Leaving the 18th green, I made a direct path to the driving range to make corrections in my swing. Every shot on the range was absolutely perfect, just as I knew it would probably be. This wasn't nerves or bad fundamentals; it was trying too hard to play well against another person.

The afternoon matches were a 180-degree turnaround. Playing incredible the entire afternoon and missing only one fairway was exactly what was needed to regain some confidence. The only problem? Pete wasn't in my group!

The only way to get past your hiccups in life is to face them head-on, and that meant my opponent Sunday morning had to be Pete. After a spectacular dinner in Spirit Hall with great stories and a lot of laughs, we returned to our cottages for the evening.

Sunday morning's weather was just as spectacular as the previous day. My warm-up session was just as good, and my confidence was soaring as we headed to the first tee. Once again, Pete hit a perfect three wood down the center of the fairway, and once again, my tee shot was the worst possible start you could have, with the ball going in the same hazard as the day before. The song "Here I Go Again" by Whitesnake came to mind immediately as my brain tried to comprehend what had just happened. The first hole was lost in match play, but my attitude was different than the previous day. The round didn't have to be horrific because of a bad start, and the reality was, it was only one hole. It was time to get focused and play the way my game had been during the Saturday afternoon match.

The front nine was a grind, with my ball getting a few crazy kicks and some wicked lies that were borderline unplayable. There was no giving up, and the match was still possible to tie for a half-point standing on the ninth tee. My tee shot hooked into the left bunker, and once again, the golf gods hated me. My ball came to rest against another lip, except this time a huge pampas bush was in front of me. Not only did my shot end up in a horrible spot but the pampas grass made my only play a pitchout. Unfortunately, the hole was lost, along with the point for team WP. My attitude was still good, but my aggravation with my finish was evident to my group as we made our way to the 10th hole.

The back nine began with a pulled drive into the left fairway bunker, and Murphy's Law showed up again. My ball had come to rest on the down slope of the tongue of the bunker. My stance was one foot in the bunker and one foot perched out of the bunker, with my hands choked down to the bottom of the grip so it would be possible to make contact. To make matters worse, Pete had hit his shot to within ten feet of the cup and was putting for birdie.

My left foot was 30 percent lower than my right as my stance settled into the white sand. With an eight iron, my shot narrowly missed the lip of the bunker and chased down the fairway, coming to rest about twenty yards from the green. The shot was as perfect as anyone could have hoped, given the lie and circumstances. With a sand wedge off a tight lie to a tucked pin over a bunker, my third shot landed softly on the firm green and came to rest six feet from the cup. Pete struck a beautiful putt, narrowly missing his birdie. My putt was a must-make, or I would lose the hole.

When my putter impacted the ball, there was no doubt it was going in. With a fist pump and sigh of relief, the back nine had started off with a small victory. The next few holes, my game was fantastic and allowed me to have a one-up lead standing on the 15th tee box.

The 15th is an island green and considered one of the most beautiful holes in Texas. Pete hit a beautiful shot to this 130-yard hole, with his ball landing pin-high as it rolled off the back of the green. This gave me a perfect opportunity to stick one close and win the hole. With a wedge in hand, my ball was pushed right, landing short in the greenside bunker. This obviously wasn't the shot envisioned, but an up-and-down should at least tie the hole.

As we made our way to the green, my ball wasn't visible in the bunker. We had all seen the ball land in the sand from the tee, so it had to be somewhere in the bunker. As we searched our, caddie motioned and said he had found the ball. Remarkably, my ball had wedged between two massive rocks that outline the bunker. I'm not sure it would even be possible to place this ball with my hand based on where it had eventually come to rest. The ball was essentially suspended between the two boulders—with no possibility of hitting a normal shot. After looking at my options for a few minutes, along with everyone in our group shaking their heads in disbelief, Pete made a comment on how he would play the shot if he had his old Bulls Eye putter. The comment changed my mind from picking up the ball and conceding the hole to pulling the my old Ping Eye 2 beryllium wedge and trying a one-handed shot. With a couple of one-handed practice swings, I made the scoop— one-handed—under the two boulders to pop the ball out and into the sand. If you gave me a hundred balls, it might not be possible to pull that one off again!

With the ball in the sand, the situation was improved but still didn't look good. The 15th green is the smallest on the course. With very little green past the pin, along with water directly behind, this made for one of the most difficult bunker shots in the game. Taking my stance and knowing what was on the line, the ball came out perfectly and landed six feet from the hole. Pete hit a poor chip, leaving a ten-foot par putt to win the hole. To my amazement, he missed the putt, and with a new lease on life, my putt found the bottom of the hole for a miraculous tie.

As we stood on the par-five 17th hole, my lead was one up on the back nine and one down for the overall match. For the first time all day, my nerves felt as if this were the first time in all our matches for me to have an opportunity to actually close out Pete for a point. Pete hit a poor drive, and the opening was there for the taking. My play was conservative, knowing a par would probably win the hole and the point for the back nine. The pin was on a shelf in the top right corner of the green. Any shot hit short would roll back down the ridge, leaving a very difficult two putt. Standing over my third shot, strategizing on how to hit the shot, the decision was made to play a knockdown shot with a cut. The shot came off perfectly, leaving me a simple two putt for par. Pete missed his par putt, and it hit me that the first full point was finally earned. Now it was time to get refocused. We were tied for the overall match, and a win on the 18th would give me a full two points out of a possible three.

My drive was absolutely ripped as the adrenaline ran through my body. Pete hit a good drive down the middle and had a hybrid into the green. He hit a great shot, but the ball didn't check and ran to the back of the green. Standing in the fairway with a wedge in hand, my shot came off perfect, landing ten feet from the hole. Pete's putt was one of the most difficult putts on the entire course. There was no way to make the putt, because the slope he was putting down would not allow the ball to travel slow enough to go in. Pete hit the putt as softly as possible, and just as I had thought, the ball gathered speed and stopped about ten feet away for par. Now, my moment had finally arrived, with the opportunity to win the match outright and collect two points for team Whispering Pines. My putt had at least three feet of break and could easily get away from me if the putt was struck too aggressively. Taking a deep breath and gripping the club lightly, I made the stroke. The ball came off the putter face perfectly, with the ball tracking on the exact line envisioned. As the ball was a few feet out, it looked like there was no way it wouldn't find the bottom of the cup. At the very last second, the ball quit breaking and stopped two feet away from the hole, securing my par. This guaranteed me one and a half points—and possibly two points—and victory over Pete if he missed his ten-foot putt for par.

Pete mentioned to me, "Nice par," as he started to place his ball on the green and remove his coin. This day wasn't about winning or beating another player; it was about testing myself and proving my game could overcome pressure. Removing my visor and extending my hand, I told Pete his putt was good, and we shook hands. At that moment, the work had paid off, as my game had finally stood up to a challenge that had ended in failure every time in the past.

Pete said some very kind words as we shook hands. He is a good friend and knew what the day had personally meant to me. We will have numerous matches in the mountains of North Carolina and the piney woods of Texas for years to come, but on this day, my game held up under the pressure of the Pete Effect.

The Rose Bowl

THERE IS NOTHING like watching a game at the Rose Bowl in Pasadena, California. The experience of a college playoff game there definitely needs to be on everyone's bucket list if your team is playing. The Oklahoma Sooners were in the playoffs and scheduled to play Georgia at the Rose Bowl. Once the game was announced, it wasn't even a question if we were going. My new motto for Christmas presents: "Building memories is more important than getting stuff."

My two kids opened their present on Christmas Day to find numerous OU shirts and nothing else. The boys looked at me a little bit in disbelief. That's all they were getting for Christmas? I asked the boys to come in the dining room, where their stockings were laying on the dining room table, covered with roses and an OU helmet. They still hadn't figured out what their big gift was until they reached in their stockings and pulled out a Rose Bowl ticket. They immediately had huge smiles on their faces and couldn't believe they were going to the big game.

Boarding the bus on January 1 from the OU host hotel was magical. We saw Baker Mayfield in the lobby, along with former coach Bob Stoops. The excitement was off the charts as we left downtown LA for Pasadena. When the bus took the Rose Bowl exit off the freeway, the anticipation started to build. I've seen the Rose Bowl so many times on television, but in person it was the most beautiful setting for a football game I've ever seen.

We were invited to the OU alumni pregame party and spent the next three hours talking to OU fans and soaking up the California sun. The Pride of Oklahoma band came into the party area at 1:00 and fired the crowd up, and then we all headed toward the stadium. Walking through the entrance tunnel, my heart started to beat like an eight-year-old on Christmas morning seeing all the packages from Santa. Walking with my boys through the tunnel, we witnessed the perfectly painted football field and mountains that created a magical 360-degree panorama view. We reached our seats, and over the next hour, we talked to everyone around us about our chances of winning.

The national anthem at the Rose Bowl was the greatest I've ever witnessed, with a Stealth Bomber flying over the stadium. It looked like something out of a Batman movie and made me so proud to be an American as the anthem came to a close. The game was set to start, and the energy level had grown to a deafening sound from both sides of the stadium. The Georgia fans were fired up, and the Oklahoma side was just as rowdy.

The game began, and Oklahoma dominated the entire first half of the game. Baker Mayfield and the offense seemed to score at will, and the Sooners looked like they were destined to play for a national championship. With only a few seconds left in the half, Oklahoma had held Georgia to 14 points when the Bulldogs decided to kick a fifty-plus field goal. This would be the longest field goal in Rose Bowl history and seemed very unlikely. One of the big mistakes OU made was not putting a player in the backfield in case the kick was short and could be returned. It turned out that Georgia wasn't going to kick the field goal until they saw the Sooners hadn't accounted for this. The ball was snapped, and history was made, with Georgia getting a momentum boost and three extra points on the board. You could feel the energy on the OU side go down significantly as the Georgia side of the field knew they had stolen three points.

If Oklahoma played the second half anything like the first half, they would be playing for the national championship the following week. Georgia had a different idea and felt like they could win the game. The Bulldogs came out in the third quarter with their running backs tearing through our defense and scoring on every play. We were stunned that our mighty Sooners were playing conservative offense when they had dominated the entire half. The coaches seemed to go in a prevent mode, instead of continuing the offensive assault they had displayed earlier. The Bulldogs dominated the third quarter and took the lead, with the Sooner defense left scrambling to come up with a stop. The Sooners offense started to click in the fourth quarter, and just like two heavyweight fighters trading punches, neither team would go down. After four quarters, the score was tied, and overtime would decide the game.

Emotionally spent and with nervousness like I've never felt, I watched the Sooners take the ball and score a field goal when they had the opportunity to go for a touchdown. Once again conservatively play-calling with the best quarterback in college football, they settled for three points, rather than going for it all and winning the game.

The next set of downs, the Sooners ran plays I've never seen them run, and they failed to get into the end zone. When Georgia blocked our field goal attempt, the game was essentially over. Georgia scored a touchdown, and the Sooner Nation sat there stunned, knowing we had let this game get away.

Any person sitting on their couch watching the first half would have assumed Oklahoma won the game if they didn't get to watch the second half. Oklahoma looked unstoppable, with the Heisman Trophy winner-to-be and the best offense in college football. Conservative play-calling and trying to protect a lead cost the Sooners a chance at a national championship. I've been to a number of championship games and have never left so distraught and emotionally sick to my stomach as I was that night in Pasadena.

On the golf course, we have all had great front-nine scores and played conservatively coming down the stretch. You can't play conservatively and shoot your best score. When you have those magical days where everything is going your way, don't put on the breaks and try to get to the clubhouse. Great players step on the gas and try to get more under par, rather than hang on. If the Sooners had taken this approach, they would've won the Rose Bowl. If you find yourself on the course this week playing great golf, get in the mindset of blowing out your opponent and shooting your lowest score. The Sooners have a great team coming back next year, but you're never guaranteed to have those kinds of opportunities. Great rounds are few and far between, so take advantage of the opportunity the next time you have a big lead at halftime, and play the back nine the same way you played the front.

The Speed Odometer

ALL OF YOU have a speed odometer in your vehicle, and hopefully, most of you haven't hit the highest speed. If you have, then you should slow down. If your speed odometer says 180 and you reach that speed, you risk having a major accident or pushing your engine to a breaking point. Either option is not good for you or your vehicle.

If you hit a driver a maximum of 270 yards, that's the distance you should plan to hit your tee shot. The problem is that most people try to hit the ball much harder than they should and usually lose consistency and distance in the process. Think of your golf swing having a speed odometer that measures total distance. Some players like Bubba Watson might have 330 yards, while players like Jordan Spieth have 280 yards on their odometer. Tour players know exactly how far they hit each club, and they don't try to squeeze more distance out of their clubs. It's very important to know how far you hit each club and choose the club needed for the intended shot.

If you are playing a hole where you can cut the corner and shave off distance to shorten the hole, but can't hit the shot far enough without swinging harder, don't try the shot. You risk having a major accident on the golf course and pushing your golf swing to the breaking point.

TrackMan and FlightScope are great ways to get your exact yardage with each club. Book a lesson with your PGA professional and ask him to track your numbers. Write down all your yardages and know exactly what club you should hit when playing a golf shot. If you don't know your maximum yardage on your speed odometer, chances are you've blown up your engine!

The Timeout

WE'VE ALL SEEN coaches call a timeout when their team starts to struggle. When the coach pulls his team off the field or court, the coach talks to them about what they need to change. Sometimes, the team is going at too fast of a pace and not focusing on running the plays correctly. There are other times where the team isn't disciplined and is going to be penalized if the coach doesn't call a timeout.

In golf, we should do the same thing and call a timeout. When you are on the driving range and you notice your swing has lost the tempo it had earlier, it's time to call a timeout. Walk away from the balls you're hitting and come back when you are able to slow down. When you are on the course and your game is unraveling, take a timeout. If you are thinking about going for the tucked pin behind the bunker and are not sure you can pull the shot off, call a timeout and reevaluate.

Coaches call timeouts for a reason, and they only get so many for each game. You've got as many as you want to take every day on the links!

The Z-Pak Theory

—— ❧ ——

EVERY SPRING, I come down with a sinus infection. My nose is stopped up, my throat hurts, my eyes itch, and I basically feel horrible. Living in east Texas wasn't the best choice for my allergies, but working at Whispering Pines makes the allergies something I can live with. Dr. Frank Smith usually gets my call every April and always knows exactly what to prescribe. When the prescription is filled, the label always reads "Take all medication as prescribed." If you don't finish the medication, it is very likely the infection will not go away or will reoccur.

Golf lessons should have the same label as prescriptions: "Take all the medication as prescribed." Most of my students continue to work on the same issues they've had for years. The reason is that they take part of the prescription and never finish their medication, like the bottle reads. They work on the flaw for a while and then move on to the next thing they want to fix in their game. When a touring professional works with his instructor, they work on very specific things to create their desired result. There is no need to work on anything else until the specific "infection" is cured.

I understand not all golfers want to spend the time working on their game like a touring professional, but what if every time you went to the range, you only worked on the move your instructor told you to work on? If you went to the range or the short game area and only worked on getting rid of a specific flaw you've had all your golfing life, you would eventually finish all the medication and become well. This is exactly what good players do, and it's what you should try to work on this year.

Think about your biggest flaw in your game and ask your instructor to address it and give you a prescription to fix the flaw. Work only on the flaw until you've taken all your medication. You can't leave any medicine in the bottle! If you do what the doctor says and follow his diagnosis, you can get rid of that nasty golf infection once and for all!

Top Hat

FOR MANY YEARS, I would take a group of members to play in a Pro-Am at Pebble Beach, Spyglass, and Spanish Bay. The Pro-Am always used the Spanish Bay Resort as the host hotel, with spectacular views of the ocean and a bagpiper playing every evening. This was such a fun event, getting to play some of the best courses in the world all in one area, and something we all looked forward to each year.

Every day leaving our hotel, we would drive past a few of the holes on the Spanish Bay course. One of the holes was named Top Hat because the green was shaped like a top hat. Mark Jones loves to gamble, so we made a bet with him two days earlier before playing our tournament round on Spanish Bay. The bet was made for a certain dollar amount that he couldn't make a six on the par-four hole. If he made a score of six, he won the bet; if he scored lower than six, he won more, and for every shot over six, he owed more. The best part about the bet was the buildup going into the round, because we passed by the hole at least four times every day. When we went to dinner, one of us would yell out, "Top Hat!" When we drove to Pebble Beach, we would yell out, "Top Hat!" It didn't matter if the radio was playing my favorite song; we would turn it off and yell, "Top Hat!" when we passed by the green.

The tournament round at Spanish Bay finally arrived, and the word of the day from the first tee until we reached the hole was—you guessed it—Top Hat. There was so much buildup as we finished each hole, and the needling was full force. When we reached Top Hat, none of us cared how our team stood in the event, only how Mark would play the hole. The hole was a dogleg to the right, with numerous bunkers in the landing zone. Each time I've played the hole, my tee shot would be a hybrid toward the left bunker, usually leaving me a nine iron into the green. Mark doesn't hit the ball very far and plays to a twenty-two handicap on average. He chose a driver and hit a low-line drive down the right side of the hole, leaving his ball directly behind a pine tree. The proper play would be a pitchout to the fairway, but that wasn't the case on this day. He tried to pull off a shot to the right of the tree and failed to get to the green. The positive of the situation was that he only laid two, with four more shots to win the bet. We all watched anxiously as he hit a Vin Scully over the back of the green for his third shot. Now, with a brutal pitch from the back of the green, he ran the risk of hitting over the green on the other side—or chunking the shot and not getting on the putting surface at all.

Mark took his time and hit an average shot (under the circumstances), leaving himself thirty feet. If Mark could two-putt this slippery downhill slider, he would win the bet, but there was a possibility of him putting off the green and making a huge number. Mark looked from each side of the hole as we laughed out loud, watching him grind over this thirty-footer. He addressed the ball and slowly pulled the putter back, and we all knew immediately he had hit the putt too hard as it raced past the hole, leaving him a six-footer. Once again, he walked to each side of the hole as we heckled him unmercifully. He addressed the putt, took two practice strokes, and stepped up to the ball for the moment of truth. His eyes looked at the hole one last time, and he stroked the putt into the cup, winning the Top Hat bet! We all cheered, laughed, and watched the color come back into Mark's face as he lifted his hands in victory.

This was a great moment with friends, but also a great way to teach my students on setting goals and playing the final hole of a tournament. I've used this numerous time with students, giving them a number they had to make on the hole and having them pay a consequence if they didn't achieve the score—or being rewarded if they made the score.

True pressure is knowing what you need to make on the hole to win. We see this all the time with tour players playing the last hole, only needing a bogey to win, and they look like they've never played golf. They hit an iron off the tee, instead of a driver, for safety and proceed to look like a twenty-two handicap playing the last hole. The irony is that the tour player is usually numerous strokes under par at this point and has played fantastic for the past seventy-one holes.

The player whose mindset changes from seeing great shots to just hanging on and playing not to lose seldom plays well! Needing a birdie to win and playing aggressively has the opposite effect. If you needed a birdie on the final hole to win your club championship, you wouldn't play conservatively; you would play aggressively. When you know the score needed to beat your buddy, remember that hanging on too tight usually results in a poor result. We all feel pressure, and this was a great way to simulate real pressure on a twenty-two handicap.

The next time you play with your foursome, make a Top Hat bet. You will absolutely feel pressure and probably feel just like Mark Jones felt on the Monterrey Peninsula that day!

How Do You Pick
the Past Two Masters Champions?

LAST YEAR, DANNY Willet won the Masters, and yours truly was holding a fifty-dollar ticket to the MGM Sports book with 65-to-1 odds. This year, yours truly was holding a fifty-dollar ticket for Sergio Garcia to win the Masters at 30-to-1 odds. I'm not sure what the odds of picking the past two Masters champions and actually pulling it off are, but here was my thinking behind the two picks.

Both Willet and Garcia were in a good place in their lives personally. Sergio has found love in Austin and even flashes the "Hook 'em" sign now and again. Danny was days away from having his first child during the Masters Tournament last year. There is nothing like falling in love and seeing nothing but rainbows and lollipops. When you find that special someone, they are all you think about, and the world seems to be in perfect alignment. And if you've been blessed to see your child born, there is absolutely nothing that can compare to that moment. God's greatest blessing is bringing life into this world through a child. Both Willet and Garcia were experiencing one of these moments during their Masters victories.

When your life is in a good place, your golf game tends to be in a better place. How many times have you rushed to the golf course with too much on your mind to really be playing, and end up having a horrible day on the links? My personal life was in shambles three years ago, and the odds of me breaking 80 were not good. Today, my world is in a much better place, and my game has been great the past year.

We can't control everything that happens to our lives, and golf and life do seem to parallel each other. I'm a very positive person, but sometimes, life can knock you down when you're not looking. Many times, these things are out of your control, and sometimes, they can be self-inflicted. With this theory, is it any wonder why Tiger's game fell apart? Swing changes and health issues played a part in his fall, but the moment his world changed, along with his golf game, was the night he crashed his SUV outside his home in Isleworth.

Sometimes, you can use tragedy or pain as inspiration and have an inner peace. Ben Crenshaw did this when Harvey Penick passed away, and he won the Masters. Davis Love won the PGA at Winged Foot after his father passed, and he earned his first and only major championship. We don't always know what's going on in a player's head and heart the week of the Masters, but I do know the past two winners had their lives in a great place that week. I'm not Nostradamus and definitely can't predict the outcome of every Masters, but the past two picks have been based on golf games that were trending in the right direction and personal lives being in a good place.

We've all heard winners of tournaments say they had calmness or an inner peace the week they won. Some players equate this to faith, and some equate this to changes in their personal lives that have brought them joy. Find more joy and happiness in your life this week, and your golf game might just get better!

Water Every Plant

———— ❈ ————

It's very possible that my gardening skills could be the worst of any golf pro on this planet. You would think that being around a perfectly conditioned golf course every day of my life would rub off on my personal lawn. Unfortunately, this has never been the case—even with well-meaning superintendents who give me advice and chemicals to help my struggling yard.

Recently, one of the workers from our club came to my house and planted a row of small trees along the back fence that borders my house. My irrigation system wasn't reaching some of the newly planted trees, so the old-fashioned way of watering was put into effect. The garden hose and twelve-dollar sprinkler from Home Depot were going to have to work. Every evening, the sprinkler was put into what seemed like the perfect position to water all the trees. As the summer started to heat up, the trees farthest away from the sprinkler were not showing the same signs of growth as the ones closest to the sprinkler. After watching my watering practice from a different angle, it became noticeable that the trees farther away were not getting as much water as the others. It wasn't intentional, but it was now obvious why these trees were dying—even though they were getting some water, they were not receiving enough to survive the Texas heat.

This made me think about how, over time, parts of our game that are neglected can start to show signs of decline, while other parts of our game receiving more attention start to flourish. If each of those trees received the same amount of water, they would all grow at the same rate. Imagine planting fourteen trees that all need water and sunlight to grow. Each of these trees represents one of your golf clubs. You need to give each club practice time, just as each tree receives water. If you looked at your practice time like this, your golf game would grow and produce at the same rate. If you were to water one tree all the time and water the other thirteen trees less, you would see one grow much higher than the others. Some golfers do this with their driver and neglect working on their putter or wedges. You might become a fantastic driver of the golf ball, but your short game would suffer. You can spend all your practice time on the putting green, which I've never witnessed anyone do, and you might become the best putter at your club. If you're the best putter at your club but can't hit a fairway or green, you're making a lot of bogey putts and not making birdies.

The moral to this story is to water each plant equally and spend equal time with all fourteen clubs—and your game will grow like a tree!

What's the Course Record?

It was a beautiful Monday afternoon at Lakeview Golf Course in Ardmore, Oklahoma. My round had started with an eagle on the 1st hole, followed by a birdie on the 2nd. Sitting at three under par after two holes, it seemed appropriate to ask what the course record was. This was absolutely putting the cart before the horse (so to speak)! My mind had already gone four hours ahead, with rainbows and lollipops floating through my head, as my scorecard would have the lowest recorded score on this golf course. You hear PGA Tour players talk all the time about staying in the present and not thinking ahead. This day, my mind and cockiness had failed miserably at staying in the present.

The only shot that matters is the shot you are about to play. It doesn't matter what you did on the last hole or will do on the next hole. Golf requires focus, and the best players in the world do this better than anyone. They are not thinking about course records if they are three under through two holes. PGA Tour players stay focused on the shot they are playing at that moment. The next time you have an incredible start to your round, make sure and stay in the present, and do not allow yourself to think ahead.

P.S. My score that day was 80!

The Y Connection

THE Y CONNECTION can be the missing link to consistent ball striking! In the first frame, you notice my arms and the club create the letter Y. Maintain this Y connection from the eight o'clock position to the four o'clock position, and you can go as hard as you want. The grip of the club always needs to point at your stomach through eight o'clock to four o'clock, while maintaining the Y connection.

Make some baby swings without using your hands to rotate the club through impact. If you maintain the Y connection and rotate properly, the face will square up perfectly at impact and release through your body rotation. As you become comfortable making baby swings, add another 25 percent and focus on keeping the Y connection at the key areas of eight to four o'clock until you can incorporate full swings.

The Y connection is a game changer for longer and more consistent ball striking!

You Don't Go to the Doctor If You Are Well

IT'S INTERESTING HOW many times a student says, "I'm so bad and beyond help." This is always the green light for me as a teacher to tell them, "Sick people go to doctors." If you are healthy, there isn't a need to see a physician. Why would you stay sick if you could see a doctor and get better? Yet golfers do this all the time! They have an unhealthy golf game that is deteriorating and refuse to get help. If your golf game is sick, go see your golf professional.

You Peek, You Miss

WHEN YOU HAVE a putt and peek, you usually miss. When the head moves, you tend to move the body, as well. Most people push putts when they peek. If you find yourself missing putts to the right, try and keep your head still for two seconds before looking. When your head stays still, your putting stroke is more consistent.

Your Past Doesn't Define You,
But Prepares You for Your Future!

MANY TOUR PLAYERS have major collapses at some point in their career. Rory McIlroy lost the Masters after his tee shot during the final round after nearly hitting the cottages left of the 10th tee. He then came back and became the best player in the world, and he went on to win numerous majors.

Jordan Spieth had the Masters won during the final round, if he played the 12th hole like he normally did. Unfortunately, he had a major meltdown, knocking numerous balls in the water and leaving him too many shots behind to recover. This could have been a career-ending mental blow, but he continued to work and believe in his game, and he won the British Open the next year.

Adam Scott had the British Open won at Royal Lytham and gave the tournament away the last two holes. I was standing on the tee when he pulled his drive left into the pot bunker, which eventually cost him the tournament. Adam persevered and won the Masters with an epic putt on the 18th the next year.

We all face challenges in life and on the course. How we react to those challenges usually determines our future success—or failure. Our golf games can't always be clicking on all cylinders, and there is only one winner in tournaments. The best players in the world only win three to four times a season. If the best players only win 10 percent of the time, then they don't win 90 percent of the time.

Don't allow a bad tournament or horrible score to define your game. Golf is full of peaks and valleys, and you might be in a valley right now, but you might be on top of the mountain the next week!